The Cricket

The Cricket: Black Music in Evolution, 1968–69

Blank Forms Editions

Brooklyn, NY

Preface

By the late 1960s, many of the Black intellectuals and artists active in the era's burgeoning arts scene found ourselves compelled by the Black Power movement rising in the South and the clarion that was Malcolm X, and we began to reintegrate ourselves into the African American communities out of which we had moved. Such reintegration was at least as visceral as it was rational: we repainted our images with enormous Afros and florid dashikis; our voices with the thought of Malcolm, primarily, but also Stokely Carmichael and H. Rap Brown; our visuals with the Kool-Aid colors of inner-city hustlers. In sum, we soaked ourselves in Blackness, in the name of cultural nationalism. The cultural nationalism broadcast from the pages of The Cricket was youthful, a proto-ideology akin to but younger than the Garveyite movement and the separatism of Elijah Muhammad. It would mature considerably when it met Pan-Africanism, but that's another story, like the song says.

Those of us who tried to speak for jazz had some very large boulders to move. The jazz press, the jazz record labels, the jazz venues were almost entirely controlled by white people, and the jazz audience was becoming whiter and whiter, in seeming contradiction to the fact that we all considered jazz to be the greatest achievement of African American people. It was, after all, the only new art music in the Western world in the twentieth century, a music so large and adaptable that it could situate itself in any culture and still retain the methods and materials from which Black Americans had made it. It was ours, we argued, and it was everywhere.

We found it intolerable that there were not even a handful of Black critics writing books, articles, reviews, liner notes, etc. So Amiri Baraka, Larry Neal, and I decided to put out The Cricket. I don't remember whose idea it was; it might have been mine, but don't quote me on that. This is a fifty-year-old recollection of a generation that is not famous for its memory. I had moved to Atlanta from New York in 1967, so Baraka and Neal did all of the actual work. We had numerous ideas on how to improve the scope and depth of the publication. The problem was that there was no budget, not even an insufficient one—you know how that goes. But the idea was good, as you can tell by the quality of the writers The Cricket attracted. With a fatter pocket, we might have gotten somewhere.

Someone should do an homage to the Gestetner mimeograph machine. It was, if not the heart, at least the vascular system of the myriad movements of the day. It was clumsy, extremely messy—you got blue ink on all of your clothes; blue ink soaked into the flesh of your hands for days. But with a mimeograph machine, a couple of reams of paper, a good stapler, you could have yourself a publication. We didn't need no stinkin' internet.

A. B. Spellman
Winter 2021

"We Need Everything": The Cricket in Context

In January 1968, Black Power!, the newspaper of the San Francisco–based Black Panther Party of Northern California, announced the imminent appearance of "A NEW BLACK MUSIC MAGAZINE":

> The Cricket is an Afro-indoamerican and Caribbean bulletin, a fast-incisive vision of where the jazz, r&b, blues, music world is, right now. . . . The Cricket will be distributed free to musicians' unions, clubs, jazz publications, record companies, schools, and will deal, as we said with ALL OF OUR MUSIC. . . . The Cricket will exist no matter what anybody thinks. We ask you to help us, if you can. Reviews, Dialogues, Interviews, Stories, Essays about our music, all of this will be part of The Cricket. . . . You decide how to respond. We need everything.[1]

Submerged in the middle of the paper, The Cricket was at once hidden away and—literally—in the center, and this positioning suggests something of the magazine's broader status and fate in subsequent years. Edited by Amiri Baraka, Larry Neal, and A. B. Spellman, four issues of The Cricket were ultimately produced between 1968 and 1969, each one longer and more expansive than the last. Though Spellman suggests that the idea for the magazine may have been his, Baraka was the driving force in its production.[2]

The Cricket was typical of the little magazines of the Black Arts and pre–Black Arts Movement era, from Umbra and Beau Cocoa to Liberator, The Free Lance, and Dasein, in its grassroots approach to production.[3] The publication was run off a Gestetner mimeograph machine in the basement of Spirit House on 33 Stirling Street, Newark, New Jersey—Baraka's residence and a headquarters for Black art, performance, and community organizing. Produced from its publishers' home, it had no budget, inconsistent production values, and limited circulation. Baraka later estimated that around five hundred copies of each issue were made, with many given away for free.[4] While five hundred people may not be enough to sustain a mass movement in any meaningful sense, it's certainly enough for the development of a thriving subculture, which might in turn spread into the broader society—just as jazz itself, in the words of Ishmael Reed, a contributor to the magazine, "jes grew."[5]

The magazine was at once local, nationwide, and internationalist. Its list of correspondents expanded with each issue, from New York and Newark to Cleveland, Chicago, DC, and LA; the fourth issue extended further still, with an essay by future South African poet laureate Willie Kgositsile on South African kwela music in the context of an apartheid state. It was also an attempt to challenge white writers' domination of criticism of Black music, and to draw attention to the economic control exerted by white club owners, label bosses, and other businessmen. As saxophonist Archie Shepp acidly put it: "You own the music, and we make it. . . . You own us in whole chunks of flesh."[6] Writing liner notes and in the pages of DownBeat, Baraka and Spellman were virtually the only Black critics on the scene, and certainly the only proponents of the New Music (the vastly unheralded Barbara Gardner, who also worked for DownBeat, wrote mainly on hard bop).

In the 1960s, when The Cricket appeared, jazz criticism—like the music itself—was at a crossroads. Jazz critics had largely been sympathetic white liberals working in a kind of ad hoc combination of amateur enthusiasm and ethnomusicology, attempting to set aesthetic criteria

(1) "A New Black Music Magazine," Black Power! 1, no. 10 (January 1968): 6.

(2) A. B. Spellman, "Preface," page 7 of this volume.

(3) For more on Black Arts publication practices, see Eugene B. Redmond, Drumvoices: The Mission of Afro-American Poetry (Garden City, NY: Anchor Press, 1976); Abby Arthur Johnson and Ronald Maberry Johnson, Propaganda and Aesthetics: The Literary Politics of African-American Magazines in the Twentieth Century (Amherst: University of Massachusetts Press, 1979); Aldon Nielsen, Black Chant: Languages of African-American Postmodernism (Cambridge, UK: Cambridge University Press, 1997); and Howard Rambsy II, The Black Arts Enterprise and the Production of African American Poetry (Ann Arbor: University of Michigan Press, 2011).

(4) Christopher Funkhouser, "On The Cricket: An Interview with Amiri Baraka," Hambone 21 (2015), 34.

(5) Ishmael Reed, Mumbo Jumbo (New York: Doubleday, 1972).

(6) Archie Shepp, "An Artist Speaks Bluntly," DownBeat 32 (December 16, 1965): 11.

from the outside. But the musicians themselves became increasingly outspoken, founding their own record labels and publishing companies and denouncing the conditions in which they were forced to ply their trade. At the same time, Baraka and Spellman emerged on the scene as Black critics of a Black music who felt fully in sync with the most radical of the new musicians. Baraka's 1963 Blues People, a remarkable history of Black music in America, concluded with an argument that the New Music was the dialectical outgrowth of an entire historical process, and one with revolutionary potential—mirroring his own turn to radical politics. From exile in Cuba, Robert F. Williams and Mabel Williams played the new jazz alongside R&B and soul on their show Radio Free Dixie, describing the musicians as "the epic poets of the Afro-American revolt."(7)

The Cricket focused primarily on the New Music: Sun Ra's photograph adorns the front cover of the first issue and the rear cover of the last, and his writing appears in all issues except for the second; much of the music discussed within was the avant-garde work of Ra, Milford Graves, Pharoah Sanders, Albert Ayler, and Ornette Coleman. Yet its conception of the Black musical vanguard was broader than any one style. As pianist Horace Tapscott put it in in the third issue, "If we had a place to play, there wouldn't be any need to classify, it'd just be people listening to their music."(8) For while white critics pointed up fault lines between different strains of Black music—particularly when the musicians were politically outspoken—Black artists had no trouble hearing them as part of the same revolutionary impulse. In 1965, Askia Muhammad Touré (Rolland Snellings) published the incendiary essay "Keep on Pushin': Rhythm and Blues as a Weapon," in which he argued for both the new jazz and R&B as tools in a cultural and political struggle taking place not just in the "ghettoes" of Black America but across what was then called the Third World.(9) Baraka took up this argument in his own "The Changing Same," the final essay in his 1967 collection Black Music, which predicted the coming of a "Unity Music": "The Black Music which is jazz and blues, religious and secular. Which is New Thing and Rhythm and Blues. The consciousness of social reevaluation and rise, a social spiritualism."(10) Spellman, too, outlined a history of Black music from work songs and spirituals through to jazz, blues, and R&B in his essay "Not Just Whistling Dixie," analyzing the forces that drove musicians out of the communities which had birthed them and urging a renewed link between the artist and the people.(11)

The Cricket unveiled its principal thesis in the first issue's editorial: "The true voices of Black Liberation have been the Black musicians. They were the first to free themselves of the concepts and sensibilities of the oppressor. The history of Black Music is a history of a peoples' attempt to define the world in their own terms."(12) Musicians were, the editors argued, "in essence the voice of a People." It's often said that jazz is the only modern art form indigenous to the United States, yet its profits had been reaped by white artists and promoters in what many musicians saw as a parallel to the extorted labor of slavery and its afterlives, from field to factory. "All segments of the white power group have benefited from the gifts of Black Music," wrote the editors. "Ofay white critics have written the histories," which, however sympathetic, come from outside the communities producing the music and inevitably "make it some other thing." Meanwhile, "recording companies have stolen the music," forcing musicians into exploitative contracts or pressuring them into compromising their art in crossover projects aimed at making their music more palatable to white audiences with greater spending power. And yet, "through all of this shit, the music has survived and propelled itself forwards."(13)

(7)
Timothy B. Tyson, Radio Free Dixie: Robert F. Williams and the Roots of Black Power (Chapel Hill: University of North Carolina Press, 1999), 285–6.

(8)
Horace Tapscott, quoted in Stanley Crouch, "Black Song West," page 101 of this volume.

(9)
Rolland Snellings, "Keep on Pushin': Rhythm and Blues as a Weapon," Liberator 5, no. 10 (October 1965): 6–8.

(10)
LeRoi Jones, Black Music (New York: William Morrow & Company, 1967), 210.

(11)
A. B. Spellman, "Not Just Whistling Dixie," in Black Fire: An Anthology of Afro-American Writing, eds. LeRoi Jones and Larry Neal (New York: William Morrow & Company, 1968), 159–68.

(12)
Editorial, "The Cricket," page 24 of this volume.

(13)
Editorial, "The Cricket," page 24 of this volume.

If the music itself survived, stronger than the economic and cultural forces that exploited or demeaned it, Baraka, Spellman, and Neal saw a possibility that the music might be linked up to broader systemic change. Such arguments were in part based on an economic analysis that understood music as another sphere of labor struggle, of struggles for representation and self-organization—discourses often couched in a fusion of socialist-oriented economics and nationalist-inflected cultural criticism. On the other hand, they adopted a visionary, quasi-spiritual register that saw music as something which, though constrained and filtered through the economic, offered something beyond it: a vision, literal or abstract, of another world. This transcendent dimension is attested to perhaps most vividly in Sun Ra's poems and poetic prose texts, couched in the language of inner and outer space, of cosmic vibrations and "alter-fate," combining autobiography, cosmological treatise, sociological speculation, and a complex, metaphor-driven theory of race.(14) These two facets also came together in the class-based registers of Black speech and the alternative forms of knowledge it contained.

In their editorial, Baraka, Neal and Spellman explained that they "call[ed] this monthly The Cricket because Buddy Bolden who is one of the fathers of Black Music had a sheet in New Orleans by that name. Bolden's Cricket has been called a 'gossip' sheet by the hip white boys."(15) Little information remains about the original Cricket; like many details of New Orleans cornetist Bolden's life and work, it's shrouded in hearsay and often scandalous rumor. As Brent Hayes Edwards notes, the very idea of its existence is based on a single paragraph in the 1939 book Jazzmen, edited by white critics Charles Edward Smith and Frederic Ramsey Jr. "In addition to running his barber shop," they wrote, Bolden "edited and published The Cricket, a scandal sheet as full of gossip as New Orleans had always been of corruption and vice. Buddy was able to scoop the field with the stories brought in by his friend, a 'spider,' also employed by the New Orleans police."(16) As Edwards notes, no copies exist of the original, and it's possible Bolden wasn't even a barber; the actual New Orleans publication called The Cricket had nothing to do with Bolden and explicitly framed itself as literary and cultural endeavor in which "politics will be of decidedly minor importance; and idle gossip of a social or other nature will be absolutely avoided."(17)

Whatever its accuracy—and Edwards's research suggests that these "hip white boys" had in fact completely inverted the truth—the idea of Bolden's Cricket remains powerful: the barbershop as a working-class social space with rumor as a form of vernacular intelligence; the musician in the community; the overlap between music, editorial practice, and self-publication. Having rightly dismissed the idea that Bolden's publication was a tabloid, the editors of the latter Cricket vowed to take word-of-mouth speculation in another direction with a regular gossip column that asked questions about the role of the music in political economy: Why did organ trios predominate over other forms of jazz in Black communities, "What is a night club? . . . . Why should our musicians play in them?," and, in a capitalized call-for-correspondence-cum-poem, wondering aloud, "DO YOU THINK THE MAFIA KILLED OTIS REDDING??????????????????????????????"

The magazine's editors were all poets first and foremost, and their writing on the new music—along with that of the musicians they commissioned, from Archie Shepp to Cecil Taylor—developed stylistically with the music itself. The essays in Baraka's Black Music, for instance, were political treatises, artistic manifestos, and prose

(14) Sun Ra, "My Music is Words," page 29 of this volume.

(15) Editorial, "The Cricket," page 25 of this volume.

(16) Charles Edward Smith and Frederic Ramsey Jr., quoted in Brent Hayes Edwards, Epistrophies: Jazz and the Literary Imagination (Cambridge, MA: Harvard University Press, 2017), 1–2.

(17) Lamar Middleton, quoted in Edwards, Epistrophies, 3.

poems drawing on the phrasing and timbre of AAVE as much as they were conventional pieces of music writing—a style epitomized in "The Changing Same." So, too, The Cricket attempted something that was in many ways entirely new: creating a form of music writing that united politics, poetry, and aesthetics as part of a broader movement for change; resisting the entire apparatus through which music is produced, received, appreciated, distributed, and written about in the Western world; going well beyond the tried-and-tested journalistic route of description, evaluation, and narration.

While Baraka, Neal, and Spellman provided the rhetorical ballast that linked the magazine to the Black Arts Movement at large, with Sun Ra supplying its visionary-philosophical element and Milford Graves its stringent insistence on the need for self-organization, it was the much more obscure musician-writer James T. "Jimmy" Stewart who furnished much of its musicological armature. Stewart, who had been part of the Muntu collective alongside Larry Neal, Charles Fuller, and Marybelle Moore, lived and played in Philadelphia for decades while working in a community center, contributing to publications such as Black Fire, The Grackle—a follow-up to The Cricket which he co-edited with Roger Riggins and Ron Welburn—and Baraka's The Black Nation. He recorded only one album, remaining virtually unknown to a broader public.[18] Stewart's writing in The Cricket burns with the same visionary zeal as the others', but he makes a more concerted attempt to ground its revolutionary calls in specific musical analysis. In this, Stewart refuses the usual division between musical analysis—understood as a distanced activity akin to the New Criticism in literature, and focused largely on Western classical music—and the political or social interpretation of the music, which is generally approached through sociology and ethnomusicology. In this, he suggests a direction for writing about the New Black Music that has, for the most part, not been pursued fully.

Stewart's comments on the relation of the non-tempered playing of Ornette Coleman and just intonation suggest a dizzyingly vast conception of music in which the Western tempered scale, oriented around the piano, came to exclude the microintervals present in most of the world's other musical cultures. Yet in the music developed by peoples of African descent enslaved in the Americas, elements of the non-tempered music survived, even as this music adapted itself to Western instruments and forms. In white musicology, these elements were described through terms such as the "blues" tone. For Stewart, however, they were more than mere secondary technical features; inserted into "the western musical complex," they were "the aesthetic evocation of a non-white people, a stylized equivalent of a distinctive tonal orientation."[19] In African American music, such elements—pentatonic scales, variable pitch—are transplanted into the piano-based pitch system of Western harmony. As Stewart argues, "The blues form like all of our musics in the West is a mixture. The over-all length and proportions is European-derived but the inner form is African."

For Stewart, the musical memory of African musical practices, transplanted to America, met and fused with European forms and instruments, not so much in the apocryphal "melting pot" but as an insurgent dialectic that could bring about an entirely new conception of music and culture. Sounding like a transformed echo of backwoods hollers, Southern blues, or the glossolalia of the Sanctified Church, New Thing musicians like Ornette Coleman stretch elements of "noise" or variable pitch to such an extent that they begin to overpower from

(18)
The album in question is Jimmy Stewart and Kuntu, An Engineer of Sounds (Cadence Jazz Records, 1984). On the Muntu collective, see James G. Spady's Larry Neal: Liberated Black Philly Poet with a Blues Streak of Mellow Wisdom (Philadelphia: PC International Press and Black History Museum UMUM Publishers, 1989), 14. Taking its name from Janheinz Jahn's 1958 book on "Neo-African culture," this group should not be confused with the musical ensemble of the same name led by Jemeel Moondoc the following decade. Scholar Pierre Crépon is conducting ongoing work into Stewart's life and writings, which it's to be hoped will appear in print soon.

(19)
James T. Stewart, "Just Intonation and the New Black Revolutionary Music," page 64 of this volume. Likewise, in an interview about The Cricket with Chris Funkhouser, Baraka recalls Paul Robeson's research into the pentatonic scale in the music of cultures from Russia to West Africa, which was gradually superseded and forced out by the Western tempered scale and its enshrinement in the piano: "I've been spreading this article around that Paul Robeson wrote on the pentatonic scale, which is mind-blowing. . . . He found the origins of pentatonic, which are worldwide. . . . At the end of the fifteenth century, a strange thing happens. As capitalism rises, the harpsichord then changed into piano and gets to be black and white notes. . . . In the harpsichord, they actually had a switch, so you could go from the old pentatonic to the new diatonic, a tempered scale that apparently the rising capitalist mind and ear of Europe dug. . . . I thought that was incredible that Robeson was studying this shit, and says, yes, that capitalism when it becomes stabilized in Europe, the piano emerges and the first thing they do is segregate the notes." Funkhouser, "On The Cricket," 36–37.

within the Western harmonic systems in which they had previously been enclosed. Parochial imaginings of European-derived musics tended, and still tend, to treat a specific, local historical lineage—that of medieval church music, say, or the invention of the piano—as the be-all and end-all of music per se. Stewart suggests that the New Black Music might at once use and move beyond what is valuable in Western music to create a new, internationalist synthesis that might be truly "universal." Much modernist European and American art had sought to renew itself by importing elements from outside Western culture: African masks, Javanese gamelan patterns, Indian rhythms and scales. But, as Stewart suggests, it was the forms from "outside" already within African American music that rendered it a Trojan horse inside the citadel of Western art, one that might even "bring down the white empire."[20]

In The Cricket's fourth issue, saxophonist Albert Ayler prophesied more than the end of a single empire—he imagined the end of the world itself. Ayler's "To Mr. Jones—I Had A Vision" combines elements reminiscent of alien abduction narratives with the mythology of the Book of Revelation and the Nation of Islam. Like his music, it is beautiful and troubling, a clarion call from a place that threatens destruction as much as it promises a new beginning, teetering on the brink of what we can conceive in the present order of things. In the same issue, Larry Neal's poetic review of Pharoah Sanders's Karma (Impulse! / ABC, 1969)—written in a style reminiscent of the great "Afro-Surreal Expressionist" Henry Dumas, murdered by a cop the previous year—likewise envisions a transfigured way of viewing time, but one that stresses ancestral continuity and the survival of the past in the present as well as the possibility for transformation within existent social forms, rather than the doing away of the present world by external forces: "The temple had a round spiraling dome and I stood with my father's spirit listening to Pharoah cascade through alcoves and spectrums of light. . . . Your brothers and sisters are there; it is sunday church picnic time in Mali or Dakar; or alabama talk, revival time perhaps. Saw you in Timbuctoo, remember? Or Chicago on 72 street."[21]

This conception of time is more than simply poetic license. Writing on Ornette Coleman's The Empty Foxhole (Blue Note, 1966)—the album in which Coleman controversially used his ten-year-old son Denardo on drums—in the second issue, Neal argued that Black artists "make or create time instead of keeping time like a metronome. 'To keep' time is a Western concept . . . if you want a more expanded universe, a multi-sided concept of time, check out drummers like Milford Graves, Rashid Ali, Beaver Harris."[22] In our temporal language, shaped by the development of modern notions of time alongside that of racial capitalism, the totalization of the work routine and the thingification of flesh, we speak about "stolen" or "borrowed" time as if time were a thing, a (private) property. Yet "increments of time contoured to abstract measure rarely match the rhythms of human action," writes Cedric Robinson.[23] Through syncopation, the chopping and changing, extending and remaking of time, Black music plays with and refutes clocking in, keeping time, being kept by time. And the alternate sense of time offered by Graves, Ali, Harris, Sunny Murray—or the young Denardo Coleman—in turn reverberates with what is out of time in The Cricket, collected here more than fifty years since its first publication.

For The Cricket was never a fait accompli. Instead, it was a beginning, a search for directions. "We must prepare our people through our art," writes Stewart in the third issue. Art, for Baraka, Neal, Spellman, Stewart, and others, was not simply a reflection or continuation of a

(20) Stewart, "The New Black Music," page 67 of this volume.

(21) Larry Neal, "Karma/Pharoah Sanders," page 124 of this volume.

(22) Larry Neal, "Further Comment on The Empty Foxhole," page 68 of this volume.

(23) Cedric J. Robinson, Black Marxism: The Making of the Black Radical Tradition (Chapel Hill: University of North Carolina Press, 2005), 177.

political line or directive, but could preempt it. At the same time, there was a tension between the argument that art might be in advance of politics—not only in tandem with it—and the more prescriptive elements of cultural nationalist aesthetics presented in the magazine—calls for "values" in the music, calls couched in often moralistic terms. "Here was the other side of the movement's protest," writes poet Lorenzo Thomas, "an urge to accomplish the moral regeneration of African American people who had been victimized and damaged by racism. Taken to an extreme, this impulse led to a rigorous, almost puritanical, concern with order and moral correctness."[24] A short review of Archie Shepp's Three for a Quarter, One for a Dime (Impulse!, 1969) by Baraka's secretary, for instance, almost totally ignored the music itself for a lengthy diatribe against Shepp's tobacco habit (the record's front cover depicts Shepp surrounded by pipe smoke). Yet, while writers—not least Baraka himself—would later critique and move away from much of the moralism of cultural nationalism, many of the fundamental concerns of The Cricket remain vital to this day: the economic and cultural control of Black music; the role of Black musicians and critics; the relation between the avant-garde and the popular; the question of how to develop aesthetic criteria for Black music separate from those of white musicology and values; and above all, how to achieve self-determination within an exploitative and often racist music industry.

This quest has been sporadically taken up in subsequent years. Though not exclusively focused on music, Baraka's newsletters and journals Unity & Struggle (1975–2007), The Black Nation (1981–86), and RAZOR (Revolutionary Art for Cultural Revolution) (1994–2004), and the performance series Kimako's Blues People (1987–2004), were, like The Cricket, grassroots initiatives nurtured within the rich local communities of Newark. And in the late 1970s, two of the Philadelphia-based writers involved with The Cricket, Roger Riggins and James T. Stewart, joined forces with Afro-Amerindian critic and poet Ron Welburn to form The Grackle: Improvised Music in Transition, publishing five irregular issues between 1976 and 1979. The magazine was a renewed attempt to form an African American and "Latin/Nuyorican" criticism, seeking to provide "sound commentary about the improvised music scene" and to "develop points of view regarding American cultural history, Afro-American nationalism, and cultural pluralism," and it contains much brilliant and thought-provoking writing.[25] Yet, as Welburn noted, critics of color rarely wrote about the music: Eileen and Joseph Southern's The Black Perspective in Music and Samuel Floyd's Black Music Research Journal, established in the 1970s and 1980s respectively, primarily concentrated on "classical" composers: "Jazz was not considered 'serious music' by anybody."[26]

The story of "Black music in evolution" after The Cricket is one of both expansion and diminishment, ripening and retrenchment and retreat. Selected musicians obtained academic positions or auspicious grants, among them Ornette Coleman, Cecil Taylor, Milford Graves, Bill Dixon, and Archie Shepp. Others found it almost impossible to survive. Albert Ayler died in 1970, his death rumored to have been at the hands of the Mafia. Giuseppi Logan, Henry Grimes, and Sonny Simmons, all of them mentioned in The Cricket, went through extended periods of homelessness; Logan and Grimes were long presumed dead before their return to the scene in the new century. And paradoxically, while ever more sophisticated and exciting fusions of popular and vernacular styles—from the "avant-gutbucket" of Coleman's Prime Time, James "Blood" Ulmer, Julius Hemphill, Ronald Shannon Jackson's The Decoding Society, Luther Thomas, and Henry Threadgill—provided ample grounds for the "unity music" that Baraka, Spellman, and Neal

(24)
Lorenzo Thomas, Don't Deny My Name: Words and Music and the Black Intellectual Tradition (Ann Arbor: University of Michigan Press, 2008), 131.

(25)
Editorial, The Grackle no. 3 (Autumn 1976): ii. "Latin/Nuyorican" is Ron Welburn's phrase. Ron Welburn, "Ain't But a Few of Us: Ron Welburn," interview by Willard Jenkins, Open Sky Jazz, August 16, 2013, https://www.openskyjazz.com/2013/08/aint-but-a-few-of-us-ron-welburn/.

(26)
Welburn, "Ain't but a Few of Us."

had sought, the general economic and cultural environment prevented such music from reaching a wider audience.[27]

In the 1980s, as Baraka argued in his collection The Music, "jazz writing, like everything else in the society . . . shifted toward the right. White chauvinism in jazz writing has in large part replaced the tentative thrust toward 'ethnomusical' and socially aware analysis . . . evident in the sixties and the seventies"—not only in self-determination journals like The Cricket and The Grackle, and in the work of writers of color like Baraka, Neal, Spellman, Stewart, Riggins, and Welburn, but via the presence of sympathetic white writers like Frank Kofsky, Robert Levin, and Nat Hentoff in DownBeat, Rolling Stone, or Jazz & Pop.[28] Increasingly, the ferment of the 1960s was seen as a political and aesthetic misstep. Of the critics associated with The Cricket, only Stanley Crouch went on to a successful career as a critic for big-circulation magazines and newspapers—and this was, one might argue, because he made a virtue of denouncing the avant-garde he once celebrated, becoming spokesman for a recuperation of jazz not as revolutionary music but as an exemplar of middle-class attainment that, in sharp contrast to the ever-present anti-imperialism of the Black Arts, was profoundly conducive to the patriotic narratives of the Reagan era, the "culture wars," and the apocalyptic triumphalism of mutually assured destruction and the Star Wars weapons program. Anthony Braxton went so far as to accuse Crouch's work of validating a "new minstrel era," involving a "narrowing of possibilities, not an expansion of possibilities" in Black art.[29] Black musicians have written brilliantly on their own and others' music, from George E. Lewis's magisterial history of the Association for the Advancement of Creative Musicians, A Power Stronger than Itself (2008), to Anthony Braxton's Tri-Axium Writings (1985), soon to be republished by New Braxton House; works by Wadada Leo Smith, Cecil Taylor, Joseph Jarman, and poet Thulani Davis (the latter two republished by Blank Forms Editions) have also received recent interest. Yet in the regular jazz criticism and journalism of long-running periodicals like DownBeat and Jazz Times—publications far more widely read by fans of the music than often-expensive academic textbooks—there are still strikingly few critics of color and a notable lack of enthusiasm for the avant-garde, which remains relegated to the margins.

Given this, The Cricket's attempt, however short-lived, at a self-determined Black criticism serves an important purpose. C. L. R. James was discussing Lenin's dialectical thought rather than the New Thing of Coleman, Ayler, or Sanders when he wrote that "the new thing LEAPS out. You do not look and see it small and growing larger. It is there, but it exists first in thought. Thought knows it is the object."[30] But his sense of the dialectical relation of intuition and systematization, spontaneity and organization—one in which the "LEAP" represents a kind of seismic jump in which everything suddenly seems possible—could well apply both to the New Thing of the 1960s and its inheritors in the years since. As Baraka wrote of the Newark Rebellion: "The spirit and feeling of the moment a rebellion breaks out is almost indescribable. Everything seems to be in zoooom motion, crashing toward some explosive manifestation. As Lenin said, time is speeded up, what takes years is done in days, in real revolution. In rebellions life goes to 156 rpm and the song is a police siren accompanying people's breathless shouts and laughter."[31]

The Cricket is an example of writers and musicians making those leaps at warp speed. Inevitably, there are misfires, missteps, directions closed down or not taken. The magazine is in some ways an ephemeral

(27) The term "avant-gutbucket" was coined by critic Jon Pareles in "Jazz Swings Back to Tradition," New York Times, June 17, 1984, Section 6, 22.

(28) Amiri Baraka and Amina Baraka, The Music: Reflections on Jazz and Blues (New York: Morrow, 1987), 190.

(29) Braxton, quoted in John Corbett, "Ism vs. Is," in Mixtery: A Festschrift for Anthony Braxton, ed. Graham Lock (Devon, UK: Stride, 1995), 198–204. For further discussion of Crouch's ideological turn, see Eric Porter, What is this Thing Called Jazz?: African American Musicians as Artists, Critics, and Activists (Berkeley: University of California Press, 2002), and Dale Chapman, The Jazz Bubble: Neoclassical Jazz in Neoliberal Culture (Oakland: University of California Press, 2018).

(30) C. L. R. James, Notes on Dialectics: Hegel, Marx, Lenin (Westport, CT: Lawrence Hill & Co., 1948), 100. For a reading of this passage, see David Marriott, " No Lords A-Leaping: Fanon, C. L. R. James, and the Politics of Invention," Humanities 3, no. 4 (2014): 517–45.

(31) Amiri Baraka, The Autobiography of LeRoi Jones (New York: Freundlich Books, 1984), 259–60.

snapshot—cheaply printed, given away or sold, part of numerous other community endeavors associated with Spirit House and Baraka's Jihad Productions. Like The Grackle ten years later and so many other exercises in avant-garde self-publishing, its ephemerality and rarity raise its mystique while also suggesting the difficulties of maintaining and sustaining artistic production against sometimes overwhelming odds. In his 1981 eulogy for Larry Neal, Baraka observed of The Cricket, simply: "Wish we had it today."(32) As the "rumors" from the past continue to reverberate in times that need them more than ever—in the words of Ronnie Gross, from the magazine's final issue, "to provide some substance for the shadow that exists"—it's important to stress that we should view The Cricket not merely as a moment in time, but as a spur to present action.(33) What we need, more than ever, is a Cricket of today.

David Grundy
February 2022

(32)
Larry Neal, Visions of a Liberated Future: Black Arts Movement Writings, ed. Michael Schwartz (New York: Thunder's Mouth Press, 1989), xii.

(33)
Ronnie Gross, "Between Shadow and Substance—Part I," page 164 of this volume.

Issue 1
(1968)

19–46

THE CRICKET

Black Music in Evolution

SUN RA - MILFORD GRAVES - TAUHID

THE CRICKET

Black Music In Evolution

Editors: Le Roi Jones, Larry Neal, A. B. Spellman

Advisors: Sun-Ra, Milford Graves

Correspondents: Gaston Neal, D. C.; Stanley Crouch, L. A.; Duncan Barber, Hilary Broadus, San Francisco; James Stewart, Philadelphia; more to come

ORDER OF ARTICLES

The true voices of Black Liberation have been the Black musicians. They were the first to free themselves from the concepts and sensibilities of the oppressor. The history of Black Music is a history of a people's attempt to define the world in their own terms. Essentially, the Black Musicians have postulated a deeply spiritual view of the world. They have been the priests of pure wisdom, in essence the voice of a People. They have paid severely for taking the role assigned to them by the demands of the Spirit. They have been fucked over by forces representing an alien sensibility, i.e. the sensibility of the Euro-American. All segments of the white power group have benefited from the gifts of Black Music. Ofay white critics have written the histories and the criticisms of our music. Slick club owners have attempted to twist the music, to make it some other thing. Recording companies have stolen the music, forcing some of our brother musicians into strange trick bags. And through all of this shit, the music has survived and propelled itself forwards into more profound areas of human experience. In sum, the Black Man's most important address to his brothers and the world has been controlled by White America.

Therefore, we propose a cultural revolution. This revolution must take place first among Black Artists. We must bring all Black Art back into the community, putting it at the core of the developing black consciousness. <u>The Cricket</u> represents an attempt to provide Black Music with a powerful historical and critical tool. In assuming this responsibility, we are saying to the world that no longer will we as Black

Men allow the white sensibility to dominate our lives. It is the responsibility of black musicians and writers to finally make a way for themselves. We know that there are those among us who do not understand the importance of the cultural revolution. These very same persons must be accused of abdicating their responsibility of Afro-American culture. They have failed to write the books and histories of African-American music and culture. They have been the victims of a deep-seated self hate, a hate which made them deny our children the knowledge of Black Culture. Where are the histories and biographies of men like Charlie Parker, Sam Cooke, Lester Young, John Coltrane, Sun Ra, Otis Redding, Duke Ellington... They are either unwritten; or when written, they are by slick would-be hip ofays who have appointed themselves guardians of Black culture. Some of the negroes who pride themselves in knowing everything Euro-American, have never heard James Brown or John Coltrane, or Cecil Taylor. They hate them black selves, sitting in the White House listening to Bernstein, never having heard Bud Powell or Herbie Nichols. _The Cricket_ advocates that the Black Artists begin to move; that we use the force of the music and the black poem (rhythm and blues) to blow them away, to blow the white thing out of them, and take control of our own thing. We must move this way. There is no culture otherwise. Only a stale hipness, that will turn itself into an inching cancer.

We call this monthly _The Cricket_ because Buddy Bolden who is one of the fathers of Black Music had a sheet in New Orleans by that name. Bolden's _Cricket_ has been called a "gossip" sheet by the hip white boys who wrote the histories. We'll have some "gossip" for the reader and a whole lot of other shit too.

MY MUSIC IS WORDS

Some people are of this world, others are not. My natural self is not of this world because this world is not of my not and nothingness, alas and happily, at last I can say this world is this unfortunate planet. The destiny of this planet is at stake, one fatal further mistake can cause its long delayed destruction. One fatal mistake can be its last mistake. The future is obvious, but the potential impossible is calling softly and knocking gently...calling softly to the natural selves of nothingness according to the standards of infinity nature and infinity nature's BEING....knocking gently upon the door of those who are of nature and natures God.

There are other dimensions and the equation of it is every other world in the infinity of the universe. This is the why of the music I represent; and this is the why of the image of a better world: the alter-life for the alter-life is different from the life of this world. This is a mean world, and by the same token, it is a poor world, poor in spiritual values, void of natural contact with the natural-infinity/otherness Being.

Suddenly, now is different from the once I knew and the things I do and say are of necessity a magnification and at the same time a nullification of calculated myths and vicar-images. Nature...intuition...psychic harmonization...NATURE...INTUITION...PSYCHIC HARMONIZATION! LIVING SYMBOLS OF DISCIPLINE...hapiness for and from the greater universe.

Because of segregation, I have only a vague knowledge of the black than I do white...I know my needs and naturalness...I know my intuition is to be what it is natural for me to be...that is the law of nature everywhere...there are different orders of being and I call upon the forces of nature to witness that I have written and I have said that no order has a right to infringe upon the rights of another order of being, for each order has its own way and weigh of being...just as each color has its own vibration....My measurement of race is rate of vibration-beams...rays ....Hence the black rays is a simple definition of itself/phonetic revelation. I do what I have to do according to my natural order of being because that is how it has to be and at the same time that is why. That is why and because; because in the scheme of things, even the least of the brothers has his day and when you realize the meaning of that day, you will feel the presence of an angel in disguise. If an angel led the exodus out of Egypt, why can't an angel lead some others somewhere else. Consider: what is the value of a dying world? Or even the life of it, if that so-called life is cruel meaninglessness...? If you do not understand anything else, understand this...that the least of the brothers in his humbleness and understanding of the weakness and the strength of everything is the initiator and the interpreter of the dimensions of the infinity...and that is why there is a black angel race of beings or soul-mates.

Freedom to me means the freedom to rise above a cruel planet. FREEDOM TO ME MEANS THE FREEDOM TO RISE ABOVE A CRUEL PLANET AND TRUE PROTECTION IS PROTECTION BY THE BROTHERS OF NATURE AND NATURES GOD...INFINITY EVERNESS....The lifting his anger and fury "a band of evil angels." ...My words are the music and my music <u>are</u> the words because it is of equation is synonym of the Living Being...darkness upon the phase of the deep...the face phase... the eye of infinity...black equation from and of the angelic is...the immeasureable ARE.

When I speak of freedom, I do not speak of the freedom of the land of liberty or the freedom of any land of this plane of existence, for this plane of existence is only a temporary illusion...shadows and images that sometimes intermingle with the delusion sent for "he sent upon them a strong delusion in order that they might believe a lie;" but and then, there is more than one lie.

The tree of the knowledge of good and evil is forbidden as far as the fruit of it is concerned but so is the tree of life. What price forbidden fruit and forbidden trees to those to whom it is forbidden? Did you ever see a voice walking? If you didn't, it is probably because you did not rea-lize the meaning and significance of the word the voice.

These are indeed perilous times. They are perilous to every man, woman or child...If the white race chooses to ignore that warning it is already of the past...Yet even now I feel a great pity for those who may not listen before it is too late....Never comes tomorrow...comes to-morrow never...tomorrow comes never...never tomorrow comes...to-morrow never comes...comes never tomorrow...there is always the alter-fate...elastic spiral potential infinity discipline other planes myth reality.

What is this world to me? it is truly nothing; I have sought to by-pass it rather than to become a part of it, because it has no known diplomatic relationships with the Creator Creater of the infinity universe. The truth concerning this planet is indeed dreadful to behold, how strange it is that the truth should reach the state of the dreadful!

Yes the truth is that the truth is bad as far as this planet is concerned. The neglected mathematics of MYTH is the equation differential potential impossible potential potential potential otherness alter-isness.

My music is words and my words are music. Why should only 144,000 understand? Yet if I am not of this world why should I care? There is great darkness and why not if they dare to obscure the name of the sun and why not if they dare to be rebellious, and why not if I have been abused and neglected and by-passed. My words are music and my music is words and none can understand better than the pure in heart, for they being pure know purity in any guise. If something or even nothing does not know its own kind, it is not being kind to itself.

My words are music and the music is words but sometimes the music is of the unsaid words concerning the things that always are to be, thus from the unsaid words which are of not because they are of those things which always are to be....nothing comes to be in order that nothing shall be because nothing from nothing leaves nothing.

The music comes from the void, the nothing, the void, in response to the burning need for something else. And that something else is something else/this nothing, this outer nothing is out of nothing, it is the music of the spheres. The symbol for every sphere is the sign of nothing: O... The spiral is another type of nothing... it is of the onward reach.

When one is primary-young... all the ideas in the world converge in counsel and through disguised declarations play upon one's brain like fingers upon some tender instrument... then there are then the impressionable days of splendor/electric naturalness/flash lightning touch upon the time negatives of variable universe and what one feels is better considered as the music of the unsaid words. That is one approach, but there are myriad approaches.

My early approach to music was in recognition of all types and forms of music as being of great importance in the scheme of order and chaos, intelligence and ignorance... the scheme of things, the general and the rare... the priceable and the priceless. To me all types of music are music but all types of music are not Space Music. According to my weigh of things: Space music is an introductory prelude to the sound of greater infinity. It is not a new thing project to me, as this kind of music is my natural being and presentation. It is a different order of sounds syncronised to the different order of Being.

I am the least of the brothers again as far as popular jazz is concerned, that is why I had the time to develop and discipline the outer-infinity coordination sound. Along the way I tried to interest popular Jazz musicians in the ideas I wanted to share with them so that we could be brothers in a pleasant as well as profitable sound venture for them as well as the listeners. They were not pioneers for the togetherness I repre-

is synonym of the Sun...after all what is there better than the expression of the you in the interplay of the self and the alter-self when the myth abstracts sound their sound.

The natural Jazz musicians I knew during my early formative years were a pleasure to know...they were sincere and unselfish.... It was always a great pleasure to hear them play for they had so many things to say in a spontaneous and natural manner, the music they played was not conventional, nor was it in popular jazz commercial form.

During my years in High School I played and studied all forms of music and the theory of same....

My relatives liked Bessie Smith, Ida Cox, Ethel Waters and other Race artists and they always took me to the theater to see and hear the Race artists perform whether they were great or small.

I believe that the first Jazz record I ever heard was by Fletcher Henderson, his records were a part of the record collection my relatives possessed. Later I added Duke Ellington, Art Tatum, Earl Hines, Fats Waller, Teddy Hill, Chick Webb, Lionel Hampton, Sunset Royals, Tiny Bradshaw, Louis Armstrong, Henry Red Allen, Jay McShann, Charlie Parker, and the other Bop greats.

Of course there were others. I used to search for everything that was new or different. There were some white bands like Boyd Raeburn and Stan Kenton until one day I found out that black arrangers were the major source of their ideas and that black arrangers and composers were BUILDING WHITE BANDS WHICH FINALLY TOOK THE

PLACE OF THE BLACK BANDS WHICH FORMERLY HAD PLAYED THE TOP JAZZ SPOTS OF THE WORLD. These arrangers probably had their reasons for doing what they did, financial perhaps...I never got around to ask them why. I do know that the black race as a whole did not wholly support what is called Jazz, they did support blues and gospel and their derivatives. Even the Negro intellectual did not seem to understand the meaning of Jazz and its contribution to the cultures of the world at large.

I appreciate all types of music but some music I find is not conducive to my development spiritually and otherwise. Basically speaking, the giants of Jazz I mentioned earlier were the musicians I listened to as a child. They had so much to say to me that I needed to hear, and in this kind of world I found that there was no one else who could say it the way they could; because all at once when they played, there was hope and happiness and natural beauty. Then something began to happen to Jazz, the Jazz musician was commercialized and packaged and Jazz began to be a product of and from the white world. In many cases, it was supervised at the recording sessions by white A and R men particularly during the reign of Bop. Since I was not a product of the white world, I found that I could not fit comfortably in the place they had reserved for the black musician. so I did not compromise and I did not lose my naturalness. What I am playing is my natural way of playing. It is of, for and to the Attributes of the Natural Being of the universe of which is, and it is to everything that should be is, because to me it is natural.

I have a gift to offer this planet and music is one of the bridges to the treasure house of it. I am doing what I am supposed to do, I am being what I came here to be. Those who are in tune with Nature can hear what those who are not in tune cannot hear, and then they will know the meaning of the natural beist. The space sea has many sounds of beistness. The Akasa, the unknown acoustics, the alter-planes of isness are all a part of everything, the everything and the nothingness of Space Outer.

Under terrific opposition, I have tried to show and demonstrate my goodwill to the world, simply because I know this can be a better world for every person, people or peoples. All that I am is a visitation and that is the meaning of the natural alter-self. If you are dissatisfied with yourself in the scheme of things and the altar has not changed conditions, perhaps you should consider the alter. After all if anything changes, it will be through the word alter/alteration/alternative because how can you dare to speak of change if you do not have an alternative? The alternative to limitation is INFINITY. Yet, be warned! Infinity is precision discipline. Infinity being INFINITY is naturally of duality because and as it is written, "The secrets of wisdom are double to that which is."

SUN RA

JANUARY 29, 1968

NEW YORK, NEW YORK

RHYTHM N BLUES

James Brown the man with a thousand Boogaloo's This brother dances all over notes with a soulful, rhythm, that has an immortal attachment to Black people. If you don't believe me check out "I Can't Stand It" or "There Was A Time."

Impressions have made the song that is a twin to "Shout Bama-lamba" by Mickey Murry, the name of it is "We're A Winner" the lyrics are telling each black person to do "like yo leaders tell you to" "I don't mind leaving here to show the world we have no fear" these brothers are telling you to tighten up and fly right. "I Wish It Would Rain," David Ruffin, Temptations are singing the Blues of today the combination of all the ajustments black people are making. Love, etc. soul music, this song is strong, rushing, and fast moving, with pluses that are in tune with every beat become part of this song. These pluses. Black people. "I Second That Emotion" Somkey says "if you feel like lovin' me "I Second That Emotion" a break and the trumpets have a strong line together. Gladys Knight & the Pips have heard a few bits of conversation. "I Heard It Through The Grapevine." "I'm In Love," Wilson Pickett. Martha & The Vandellas, "Honey Chile." Five Stair steps & cubie "Something Missing." The O' Jay's, "I'll Be Sweeter Tomorrow."

Larry A. Miller

ONE. IN A SERIES

White. musicians play, like old cracker janitors.

Trying to open schools, (with the wrong keys).

No beat, no style a blank/nothingness.

instruments become peanut butter sandwiches on

Hot deserts. They become Tony Bennetts, Al Jolsons, Bill Cosbys,

Singing to dead shadows, that masturbate on

nothingness, but some of you dig it.

Larry A. Miller

MILFORD GRAVES

THE BLACK MUSICIAN MUST REALIZE HIS EXISTENCE AS A CREATIVE FORCE WITH A DETERMINED EMPHASIS ON WHO AM I, AND WHAT IS MY POSITION IN THE PRESENT SOCIETY THAT SURROUNDS ME. IF ALL BLACK MUSICIANS WERE REALLY AWARE OF WHAT'S HAPPENING TO HIM, THE CRUEL OPPRESSION THAT SMOTHERS HIS GENIUS, WE WOULD BY ALL MEANS HAVE A UNITED BLACK MUSICIANS FRONT. MANY BLACK MUSICIANS CLAIM TO KNOW OF THE EXPLOITATION THAT HAS ENSLAVED HIM, BUT FEW HAVE INVOLVED THEMSELVES IN A SELF RELIANCE PROGRAM. IT SEEMS THAT THE OUTLOOK OF THE MAJORITY OF BLACK MUSICIANS TODAY IS TO REFRAIN FROM A BUSINESS KNOWLEDGE, HAVE A EXTERNAL SOURCE (IN THIS PARTICULAR CASE THE EXTERNAL SOURCE IS THE WHITE-WESTERN EXPLOITER) MAP OUT YOUR ECONOMIC SURVIVAL, WHILE YOU LOOSE YOURSELF IN THE MUSIC. THIS IS DIRECT MENTAL SUFFERING PLUS ABSTENTION FROM ECONOMIC POWER FOR THE BLACK MUSICIAN. IF WE CHECK THE SCENE TODAY WE HAVE TWO CATEGORIES THAT THE BLACK MUSICIAN MAY BE CLASSED INTO. ONE CLASS WE CAN CALL THE PUBLICISED-NO MONEY BLACK MUSICIAN AND THE OTHER CLASS THE PUBLICISED-CHUMP CHANGE BLACK MUSICIAN. THE BLACK MUSICIAN IN THE PUBLICISED-NO MONEY CLASS WILL IN MANY CASES PROSTITUTE HIMSELF IN ORDER TO SURVIVE. THERE IS NO NEED TO DO THIS IF YOU ACCEPT AND BELIEVE IN YOUR SELF AND BLACK BROTHERS. HOW MANY BLACK MUSICIANS ARE WALKING AROUND WITH AN ABUNDANCE OF PEOPLE SAYING---I KNOW HIM, HE IS SO AND SO, AND AT THE SAME TIME YOUR UNAWAKENED SELF IS FULL OF IGNORANT SELF ESTEEM. BUT ONCE THESE TRICK WORDS THAT THE EXPLOITER HAS REWARDED YOU DISAPPEARS, YOUR TRUE CONDITION ARISES ONCE AGAIN, YOUR UPTIGHTNESS FOR THE MUCH NEEDED MONEY-ECONOMIC COMFORT. IF YOU LACK THIS YOUR NATURAL GENIUS WILL GRADUALLY DIE. THE BLACK MUSICIAN MUST REALIZE THAT WE ARE THE RAW MATERIAL THAT THE EXPLOITER MUST HAVE FOR HIS FINISHED PRODUCT AS A PROFIT MAKER. WE MUST PRODUCE OURSELVES FOR A POSITIVE MUSIC AND ECONOMIC SURVIVAL. IF YOU VALUE YOURSELF AND WANT TO FURTHER PROGRESS YOUR MUSICAL GENIUS FREE OF SELF DESTRUCTION WHICH WE HAVE ENCOUNTERED FOR SUCH A LONG TIME, THAN UNIT, UNDERSTAND BUSINESS PROCEDURE, AND BECOME SELF-RELIANT. NOW WE CAN PROCEED TO CHECK OUT THE SECOND CLASS THE PUBLICISED-CHUMP CHANGE MAKING BLACK MUSICIAN (SOME BLACK MUSICIANS MAY FALL INTO A HIGHER LEVEL AMONG THIS CLASS. THIS IS A DANGER LEVEL, BECAUSE THE WHITE-WESTERN EXPLOITER BECOMES MORE CONCERNED TOWARDS YOUR POTENTIAL ECONOMIC POWER). ASK YOURSELF WITH TRUE HONESTY SUCH QUESTIONS AS, HOW LONG DID IT TAKE ME TO MAKE

THIS CHUMP CHANGE, AND UNDER WHAT CONDITIONS WERE I TO COMPROMISE. YES, CHUMP CHANGE COMPARED WITH THE WHITE MUSICIANS INFINITE AMOUNT. THESE ARE THE SAME WHITE MUSICIANS THAT STOLE FROM YOU, THAT AT ONE TIME OR ANOTHER TRIED TO HANG OUT AND COMMUNICATE VIA SOUL TALK. FOR THE BLACK BROTHER WHO COULDN'T SEE THROUGH THIS ARTIFICIAL IMAGE, HE WAS THE VICTIM OF A HISTORICAL THIEF. HE WAS TO HAVE HIS MUSICAL CREATIVENESS AND NATURAL ENERGY SUCKED DESPERATELY FROM HIM. IF THIS WHITE MUSICIAN WAS SO DEDICATED TO YOUR MUSICAL GENIUS AS HE SO HUMBLY ADMITS DURING HIS HANGING OUT PERIOD, IT SHOULD BY ALL MEANS MANIFEST ITSELF ON A INFINITE EXISTENCE WHEREAS THE BLACK MUSICIAN WILL PROSPER. THE WHITE MUSICIAN HAS FALSELY GIVEN THE IMPRESSION OF HIS CONCERN OF YOU BEING THE BENEFACTOR FROM YOUR MUSICAL GENIUS. HIS ONLY DEDICATION IS TO STEAL FROM YOU, TO TELL YOU HOW GREAT YOU ARE, AND THE RECOGNITION AND ECONOMIC COMFORT YOU SHOULD HAVE. BUT TELL ME BROTHER DO YOU HEAR THESE WORDS ONCE THE WHITE MUSICIAN HAS EXTRACTED FROM YOU THE ENERGY NEEDED TO ACTIVATE YOUR MUSICAL GENIUS. NO, THE ONLY WORDS YOU HEAR FROM HIM ONCE HE IS IN HIS HARD WANTED POSITION IS COME WORK FOR ME, HE MAY CALL YOU FOR A GIG, NOW HE HAS REVERSED THINGS HE WILL TELL YOU WHAT TO PLAY. WHAT HE WILL BE ACTUALLY DOING IS TELLING YOU WHAT YOU TAUGHT HIM IN A DIFFERENT WAY. IF HE REALLY MEANT HIS DEDICATION IT WOULD'T CHANGE, HE WOULD IN ALL RESPECT GRANT YOU WHAT HE HAS THAT YOU RIGHTFULLY DESERVE. THESE ARE THE WHITE MUSICIANS THAT YOU HAVE HUMBLED YOURSELF TO SO THAT THEY CAN FURTHER EXPLOIT YOUR MUSICAL GENIUS IN EXCHANGE FOR CHUMP CHANGE OR MENTAL DEPRESSION FROM UNHEALTHY ACTS FOR THOSE WHO CAN'T MUSICALLY SURVIVE. WAKE UP BLACK MUSICIAN AND UNITE FOR ECONOMIC CONTROL OF YOUR MUSICAL GENIUS. LET'S CHECK OUT THE TIME FACTOR THAT'S INVOLVED IN REACHING YOUR CHUMP CHANGE POSITION. AS WE KNOW OUR ENDEAVOR TO PORTRAY OUR MUSICAL CREATIVENESS BEGINS AT A YOUNG AGE. THIS IS A PRIMARY STAGE IN OUR CREATIVE GROWTH, A TIME WHEN ECONOMICALLY BEING COMFORTABLE IS VITAL TO OUR MUSICAL GENIUS. WELL FOR MANY BLACK BROTHERS IT TOOK YEARS TO MAKE THIS CHUMP CHANGE A TIME WHEN YOU ARE WEAKENED FROM TOO MUCH DISSIPATION. THE TIME INTERVAL DURING THIS PERIOD WE ARE TOLD IS ONE OF PAYING YOUR DUES. IN REALITY WE HAVE BEEN PAYING DUES ALL OF OUR LIFE, BUT THE MUSIC PAYING DUES IS FOR A SPECIAL REASON. THIS IS THE PERIOD WHEN THE WHITE-WESTERN EXPLOITER WILL HAVE HIS PLAN IN FULL OPERATION. THIS IS A PERIOD WHEN THE BLACK MANS GENIUS WILL BE SUCKED FROM HIM. A FAILURE TO REALIZE AND UNDERSTAND WHAT SELF-HELP IS WILL CAUSE THE BLACK MUSICIAN TO PAY THESE UNNECESSARY AND VERY

IGNORANT DUES. PROPAGANDA IS CONSTANTLY THROWN AT YOU TO SUPPRESS ANY THOUGHTS THAT ARE CONVICTIONAL FOR YOUR REALIZATION OF THE FALSITY OF THE PAYING THE DUES CONCEPT THE BLACK MUSICIAN MUST AWAKEN HIMSELF TO THE FACT THAT HE IS THE TEACHER AND THE WHITE MUSICIAN IS THE PUPIL DURING THIS SO-CALLED PAYING THE DUES PERIOD----THAT THE PROPAGANDA USED ON YOU IS TO MAKE YOU BELIEVE THAT YOU AND THE WHITE MUSICIAN ARE EXISTING ECONOMICALLY ON A EQUAL BASIS. THIS IS TO COOL YOU OUT, TO MAKE YOUR ATTITUDE TOWARDS THE WHITE MUSICIAN BE WHEREAS HIS REJECTION LIKE YOURS WILL CAUSE YOU TO ACCEPT HIM. THIS IS MASTER PSYCHOLOGICAL STRATEGY. BUT CHECK THIS OUT THEY NEVER SAY EQUAL MUSICAL ABILITY DURING THIS SO-CALLED PAYING THE DUES PERIOD. IF THE SO-CALLED WESTERN AUTHORITATIVE SOURCES (MUSIC CRITICS) SAID THIS IT WOULD CAUSE A MISCONCEPTION WHEREAS THE WHITE MUSICIAN WOULD RELAX HIS DESPERATENESS OF EVENTUALLY GAINING CONTROL OF YOU WHEREAS IT WOULD BE ADVANTAGEOUS TO HIM. BUT ADVANTAGEOUS IN WHAT RESPECT? TO FULLY UNDERSTAND HOW THE WHITE-WESTERN EXPLOITER BENEFITS YOU MUST WITH STRONG INTERNAL AWARENESS LOOK AND LISTEN TO YOURSELF NOW AND COMPARE IT WITH YOUR YOUNGER-ENERGETIC NATURAL SELF. IN ALL PROBABILITY IF YOU HAVE PLAYED THE WESTERN EXPLOITERS GAME OF WESTERN INTELLECTUALISM, USED HIS DERIVED AT SYMBOLICS FOR MUSICAL REFERENCE, YOU WILL REGRESS TO A STATE WHEREAS YOU WILL BE A PASSIVE-KNOWLEDGE GIVING FORCE. IF JAZZ WAS FREE OF WESTERN MUSICAL SYMBOLICS (USE YOUR OWN), THE WHITE MUSICIAN WOULDN'T GAIN ECONOMIC POWER FROM HIS PLAYING AND UTILIZATION OF JAZZ. THE BLENDING OF WESTERN MUSICAL THEORY WITH BLACK RHYTHM ONLY SERVES TO DIRECT AND FORM HIS THEORY INTO A MUSIC THAT WILL HAVE A STRONG APPEAL ON THE PEOPLE. DON'T FORGET RHYTHM IS THE MOTIVATING FORCE OF MUSIC. THE NEW BLACK REVOLUTIONARY MUSIC IS COMPLETELY FREE OF WESTERN THOUGHT, IT INVOLVES THE PRINCIPLE THAT THE WESTERN-EXPLOITER HAS STOLEN THROUGHOUT HISTORY-THIS BEING NATURAL CREATIVITY. BUT ISN'T A MUSIC THAT IS A BLEND, THAT HAS UNIVERSAL APPEAL SOMETHING GOOD? YES IT IS IF WE BENEFIT FROM IT MUSICALLY AND ECONOMICALLY SINCE WE ARE THE MASTER ARCHITECT IN JAZZ CONSTRUCTION. BUT ARE WE THE BENEFICIARIES IN JAZZ? NO. THE WHITE MUSICIAN BENEFITS THE MOST MUSICALLY AND ECONOMICALLY. WITH THE BLACK MUSICIAN CONSTANTLY GIVING HIM CREATIVE KNOWLEDGE, THIS BEING POSSIBLE BECAUSE OF THE WHITE EXPLOITERS TRICKOLOGY. WHEN YOU HIRE HIM YOU ARE ONLY GIVING HIM PUBLIC ENDORSEMENT, AND MOST OF ALL YOU ARE TEACHING HIM. THIS WILL ALL BE USED AGAINST YOU BY THE WHITE MUSICIAN FOR HIS SURVIVAL ONCE HE FEELS HE HAS CONTROL OF THE SITUATION TO ORGANIZE JAZZ WHEREAS HE MAY OR MAY NOT NEED YOU UNLESS A NEW MUSIC COMES ON THE

SCENE, SUCH AS THE NEW BLACK REVOLUTIONARY MUSIC. HISTORY AS WELL AS THE SO-CALLED WESTERN AUTHORITIES ADMITS THAT THE ONLY TRUE ART FORM IN AMERICA, JAZZ, WAS CREATED BY THE BLACKMAN. THIS ACKNOWLEDGEMENT ALONE WILL TELL YOU THAT YOU ARE THE TEACHER, SINCE JAZZ CAN ONLY BE TAUGHT FROM A HUMAN STANDPOINT AND IS A NATURAL FUNCTION WITHIN THE BLACKMANS LIFE EXPERIENCE. BLACK MUSIC IS A LIVING AND EXPERIENCED MUSIC AND NOT ONE TO BE STUDIED FROM ANY WESTERN INTELLECTUAL SOURCE (TEXTBOOKS, SCHOOLS), THAT THE ONLY SOURCE IS THROUGH ACTUAL SPONTANEOUS-IMPROVISED PARTICIPATION AMONG OUR FELLOW BLACK BROTHERS TO POSITIVELY ASSEMBLE AND DIRECT OUR FEELING-VISIONS THAT WE HAVE EXPERIENCED IN LIFE. THIS WILL ANSWER THE PROPAGANDA OF THE WHITE MUSICIANS EQUAL ECONOMIC STATUS---THE WHITE MUSICIAN FEELS HE MUST GO THROUGH THIS PERIOD (HE WILL TRY TO EXPERIENCE THE BLACK MUSICIANS LIFE) TO UNDERSTAND THE FUNDAMENTAL FEELINGS INVOLVED IN BLACK MUSIC. IN TRUE REALITY THIS ORDEAL THAT THE WHITE MUSICIAN FELT WOULD PROVIDE HIM WITH THE FUNDAMENTAL FEELING NECESSARY FOR JAZZ DIDN'T WORK. IT IS VERY IMPORTANT TO UNDERSTAND HOW ANOTHER SCHEME WAS DEVISED TO CAPTURE THE BLACK MUSICIANS GENIUS. WE COULD GO BACK HUNDREDS OF YEARS AGO, BUT LET'S START FROM THE NEW ORLEANS PERIOD, THE TIME WHEN THE SEED WAS MATURING FOR A NEW BLACK MUSIC. THIS IS A PERIOD THAT THE BLACK MUSICIAN MUST STUDY TO UNDERSTAND HOW HIS MUSICAL GENIUS WAS TO BE MOLDED---HOW YOU WERE, ACCORDING TO THE WESTERN-EXPLOITERS SCHEME TO PIECE TOGETHER A WESTERN DEVISED THEORY, WHEREAS YOU WERE BEING TRICKED TO TEACH AND GIVE THE WHITE MUSICIAN A MUSICAL DIRECTION, AND AT THE SAME TIME FOR YOU TO REGRESS FROM YOUR NATURAL-INNATE CREATIVE ABILITY. THIS WOULD EVENTUALLY LEAVE YOU IN A STATE OF TOTAL MANIPULATION, WHEREAS YOU WOULD NOT BE THE MANIPULATOR, BUT THE MANIPULATED. THE HISTORY OF THE BLACK MUSICIANS PLIGHT IN MUSIC ON A ECONOMIC BASIS SHOULD SERVE AS A INCENTIVE TO BECOME SELF-RELIANT.

And some music is not music
But some notness is noteness
Sound of the realm not
Otherness.

One day you will see
That thatness
Through the image of the eye
And the multi-I of the council of the I's.

One day
Not once
But hence
Thence
There
Other where
Twice the day
Twice
Twice before the time
And....And....
Twice above....beyond....below
Eternal....twice
Never with the remembrance of once
Once
Never upon a time
Twice Twice
You will see that thatness
Thereness....Theirness....themness

Light birds lighting land
Upon the land birds light
And the light is as the darkness
Within they dwell the land.

Through the eye
The sound has spoken thatness
This is
And my thatness

Sun-Ra

TAUHID Impulse A-9138 Pharoah Sanders, T; Sonny Sharock, G; Dave Burrell, P; Henry Grimes, B; Roger Blank, D

is the young pharoah still coming through the desert to claim what I think will be his. His birthrite, as left to him, by Trane, his own true father.

Certainly we know that it is about honor, and the being accepted in whatever place our own energy (awareness of God) commits us to. With Trane's passing, we all look for the creator who will truly use the heaven of sound left out here by that man.

On Upper and Lower Egypt Pharoah just about gets off. The conception is so beautiful, and that funky earth noise ("tune") he has carrying him sweeps along all our feeling for completion. The scream in the midst of that long line, is the feeling for sublime direction in the midst of the constant business of looking waking breathing working, &c. Our old symbol the phoenix, it too from Egypt, is what that sound finally makes me think of, that black bird bursting out of flame. The ending of the Japan side (Venus-Capricorn Rising) is a replacing, a restating, of what is now the known contemporary black emotion. The bursting, the flight, the screaming.

But Pharoah has a mastery of tone, you can hear in person, he hasn't to my knowledge yet recorded. A mastery of "harmonics," a breath control...to draw out the sound into infinitely sounded slivers of feeling. This is what we look for. The completion the rounding into "completness," with the whole battery blowing out. Pharoah has incredible power, and incredible tenderness soulfulness...like a love of playing, of sound, that will spread your consciousness dazzled among his notes.

The man's voice sound is also beautiful and important on this side. The human sound of the feeling. Only Sun-Ra and Trane have gotten into using their voices...Ra most heavily with his songs, and hipditties "Nest Stap Jupider..." Pharoah bringing the single directed voice into play. The presence of the presence, the human "behind" the blowing. Get off them machines a second brothers, let us know whose there. Sing something hip or weird or intelligent or about how to raise the race.

Guitarist Sonny Sharock is the heaviest thing I've heard on that instrument since them dudes that used to put broken bottle necks through the necks of the guitar and scream like muhfuhs. He really has something strong and black going, for definite. The rest of the band is good, I hope Pharoah can keep them together, Burrell I heard, setting up alot of the runs, with a deeper McCoy like lyricism. Roger Blank and Henry Grimes compose the rhythm section of anybody's dream band. Henry, "5stars" for everything he do, he do it so good.

To Pharoah/Cricket prays him the continuing strength necessary to play all of the wonderful music we all know is in him.

JIHAD (PUBLISHERS OF THE CRICKET)

MANIFESTATIONS OF THE BLACK SOUL
(Spirit Forces- Purple Magic Men Invade

THESE ARE SOME OF OUR NEW FLAGS!!!!!!

BOOKS * RECORDS * FILM * DRAMA (Write for information re:SPIRIT HOUSE MOVERS/ We bring Black Drama anywhere)

BOOKS

AFRO ARTS ANTHOLOGY...... New Work by Larry Neal, Q.R. Hand, Ben Caldwell, LeRoi Jones, David Henderson, Sonia Sanchez, Joe White, Ed Spriggs, Yusef Iman, anonymous yellers.... $1.00

BLACK ART.... New Poems by LeRoi Jones $1.00

SLAVESHIP.... A one-act play by LeRoi Jones $1.00

BLACK WOMAN'S ROLE IN THE REVOLUTION ...... A much needed redefining of why and how the "The Queen Of The World" must function NOW, and in the coming struggle. $1.00

ARM YRSELF OR HARM YRSELF ... A one-act play by LeRoi Jones $1.00

THE MILITANT PREACHER... A play by Ben Caldwell...................... $1.00

PRAISE THE LORD BUT PASS THE AMMO.... A play by Yusef Iman $1.00

SOMETHING BLACK.... poems by Yusef Iman $1.00

BLACK REVOLUTIONARY SONGS .... by Yusef Iman $1.00

FILMS/

BLACK SPRING .... A documentary of the Black Arts Alliance travels on the West Coast, Spring 1967. Features: Rap Brown, Huey Newton, LeRoi Jones, Maulana Karenga, Floyd McKissick, ... Rental $50.00

DUTCHMAN .... A film based on the award winning play by LeRoi Jones .... Rental $100.

RECORDS/

BLACK & BEAUTIFUL... Soul Music full of Black Power. Yusef Iman, The Jihad Singers, LeRoi Jones, reading. 33rpm LP $5.00
45rpm EP $1.00

SONNY'S TIME NOW ... SONNY MURRAY drums, Albert Ayler, tenor; Don Cherry, trumpet; Henry Grimes, bass, Louis Worrell, bass; LeRoi Jones reading "Black Art".... $5.00

jihad productions ..... box663 NEWARK, NEW JERSEY

EXPLOITATION BLUES!
HOW'M I DOIN', NORM?
THE PUBLIC'S NOT READY FOR YOU YET —WE'RE NOT MAKIN' A DIME! KEEP PLAYIN'!
BLACK MUSIC

Issue 2
(1968)

47–72

THE CRICKET II

CONTENTS PAGE

THE CRICKET

Black Music In Evolution

Editors: Le Roi Jones, Larry Neal, A. B. Spellman

Advisors: Sun-Ra, Milford Graves

Correspondents: Gaston Neal, D. C.; Stanley Crouch, L. A.; Duncan Barber, Hilary Broadus, San Francisco; James Stewart, Philadelphia; more to come

ORDER OF ARTICLES — Page

We're A Winner is what Bro Jones was talking about in Black Music. The blues impulse given social thrust and revolutionary intelligence. All our arts are not arts unless they be the total meaning of men, express the grandest design of human life, the striving of humans for rational loving life on this planet and the next.

"Do what your leaders tell you to", the next question, let us let all leaders, as chief brother, says, "have leading information". That goes for James Brown as well as Whiteknee Young. "I dont mind leaving here to show the world we have no fear", is the correct religious belief. Black people heir to the richest part of the world, all ways.

Address ourselves to absolute reality, imagination is for changing reality. Use it, that way. New image of what ought to be. Build here! Dig there! Reconstruct a world, if it aint what you want.

All our art must do this, or show why it need to be done. Look, the next time anybody see James Brown or Invisible William, tell 'em to sing or blow some new black music. Le's get somethin goin. Get them words <u>right</u> and righteous, brother...and you horn players, dig it, when you be into some corny shit, it <u>do</u> show in yr playin...cause you be usin and describin parts of the energy that are negative attitude. That's the only reason the Andrew Sisters sound like they do, they be describing somethin awful which they is any way. Watch out fast and slick and rough niggahs, theres a fast and slick and rough nigga fakeout machine, TOO. You wake up one day like a cat in bro jones play, won so many academy awards, and invisible tiny blanco fairies be slidin in and out midnight yo bed lumpy behind it, that one day you wake up (the name of this is THE SIDNEY POTER TRAGICAL)... ... and the sounds you be makin beees UGLY

WHAT. YEH NO SHIT--HE WOKE UP ONE MEWNIN COLD ASS WHITE!!

EDITORIAL

BLACK SONG WEST

by Stanley Crouch

Believe it if you want to, but Los Angeles is not so much a decadent city musically as the jazz press here is decadent. There are many men who can play. Many. But to read the popular music journals like JAZZ or Down Beat, one would believe the only players out here are Don Ellis (the watchmaker) and Tom Scott (a boy who couldn't even hear the clear connections in the extended work of Don Cherry's COMPLETE COMMUNION which he reviewed for JAZZ). That's all fantasy. There *are* musicians here, and I would like to introduce one of the groups in this first column which is the result of a conversation with its leaders.

The New Art Jazz Ensemble

In the underground of Old New York when Ornette Coleman was still "new", one of the trumpet players taking the music away from where it had been was Bobby Bradford. He disappeared after cutting a record with Coleman for Atlantic in 1962 which was never released. He's in Los Angeles now, and has formed a group with reedman John Carter: The New Art Jazz Ensemble. Bradford still plays trumpet, Carter alto and tenor saxophones as well as clarinet (the ensemble sound with Bradford's trumpet beside that clarinet is a *gas*), Tom Williamson is the bassist and Bruz Freeman the drummer.

Carter and Bradford formed the band in the summer of 1966 when the trumpeter was living in Pomona and Carter in Los Angeles (a good

30 miles apart). Since then the personnel has changed, the piano that was there when it was a quintet has disappeared, and they now have what they want to work with--though, like many musicians in America, they all have day jobs, but, they say, this is a help of a sort.

"It's not a happy thing," says Bradford, "but we're working toward making a living playing. So, since we all work day jobs, we don't have to cater to a club owner or a particular audience for that twentyfive dollars a night thing."

"The whole purpose," adds Carter, "is to make good music."

"That's the kick," Bradford continued, "not to cater to club owners or a & r men or anybody--though no a&r men or anybody else is asking us to do anything but go to hell. At the moment."

But whether anybody likes it or not, they know what they're doing, have been through the other things: Bebop, R & B, standard tunes, got <u>that</u> down, and are now accepting the heavier responsibility: Honesty.

Carter puts it this way: "The idea of being true to the art means to me the artist trying to convey the true thing of himself to the listener. The difference between trying to sell and trying to project something truly felt is the difference between being true to the art and being commercial. You see, our basic purpose is no different from that of any other jazz group. Our aim is to explore any tune to the greatest extent possible at the moment we're doing it. We hope that in our exploring of any tune the result will be good jazz. Our improvisation is in free form, and, basically, I feel, like Bob feels, there is no reason a player should be hung up with chordal progressions. He should be able to play whatever he wants in a particular musical setting. That takes care of the whole pie. All we do then is play what we deem most musical for that particular thing."

Bradford broke it down to this: "I could never see myself going up on the bandstand playing something I didn't want to play, didn't like, and had no relationship to me whatsoever. Playing is mile-a-minute decisions, that's how I see it. An encounter with myself. When I win, it's a groove, but, I can never lose. That is, I don't get all the little things, but a picture has been painted. I see it as a problem, and all problems in my mind have a solution. Doors open, but a cat has done nothing if he can't get past what's already prepared for him. I mean Duke Ellington or Billy Strayhorn can provide a beautiful tune to get you over to the listener, but it's better when you're on your own. The beauty of what we doing, to me, is we use our own tunes, and whatever we come up with <u>we've</u> done. What we achieve is of our own making. You can, you dig, have good material though, and have a lousy group. But whenever we do something good, it's our own, nobody else's."

He went on to say that he is interested in coming up with songs that will keep the musicians from regressing to a point of playing things they already know ("I want the music to go <u>forward!</u>"), is interested in continually learning new things about music and about his instrument, and considers songs as ways of setting up moods that will convey certain things to an audience. "Like to me, modal, not in the strict musical sense, can be about moods." "Yes," Carter added, "we try to play so that anybody can lead the way if what he's playing is strong enough. A change of mood, a different tempo or a different feeling, but, with everybody else so that the tune, whatever you do to it and wherever you take it, from start to finish, is not head, solos head, but one total thing."

That is, musical taste. Nobody leaning on anybody else or being carried along on the strength of the others' abilities. That, they pointed out, is more demanding on each player's sensitivity and creative ability, no laying flaked out on standard grooves.

"We can't coast," says Bradford, "that's why it's so taxing mentally and physically."

And they don't coast. When I heard them in rehearsal I almost immediately wondered how well this band would do were it in New York--as far as recognition is concerned, since we all know there's no money no place, no big money unless you become a Black Hippie like Charles Lloyd or play rock tunes accompanied by strings and corny choral groups. Hardly any place to make it unless the Black Communities in all our cities are awakened, places are found to play in for extended periods so that audiences can develop--I mean some place for the music to be for MONTHS so that the artists can establish that particular place as THE PLACE TO BE. That's all Bradford and Carter's band needs, because they have got a way that's not anybody else's. The songs they play are unusual, their ensemble sound is not that of the usual brass-reed combination because Bradford has some kind of a way of giving his horn a color that will match whatever reed he's next to, and can solo his ass off! The lines he plays seem to skip through the bar lines and outside the rhythm in a way that makes his horn seem "above" it. The sound of his horn is big and way away from the sound the others make, and he is very much the melodist who can some way make a quote from something like "Salt Peanuts" fit the music of today. Trumpet players should look for him so they can listen to something. And Bruz Freeman keeps the rhythm going like a pendulum unevenly circling then falling for a second to a set thing then moving away then putting it all together. A solo he took on a song they call "Sticks & Stones" had that natural but uneven flow of the ocean, the surf, which he achieved by widening and shortening his rolls in unexpected places then accenting them with Africx paradiddles then playing his cymbals in a way that made their overtones blend and meld into each other. It was a hell of a solo--and he was SICK! having just recovered, or in the process of recovering, from an automobile accident. Tom Williamson, as opposed to a lot of bass players, doesn't play a bunch of notes, makes the time elastic, the sound large, and bounces beautifully against Freeman's drums. Carter reminds me of a little mad black maniac, his solos have so much humor, but then poise, seriousness, giggles. Just dig him.

It may be the very serious lack of maliciousness that makes this group so beautiful: The LOVE for the music, as Milford Graves says,

"When the musicians will know nothing but music. Nothing but music."

Hear this group. And any clubowners should contact JOHN CARTER at 757-1197 if they're interested in hearing a different kind of music in Los Angeles.

****

TO OTIS

TO OTIS REDDING
whose voice carried me to the hearts
of my brothers
and, "i don't wanna' stop now."

TO OTIS REDDING'S SOUL
immortalizing the blackman's arms
around his woman

TO OTIS REDDING
BIG, BLACK AND DEAD. killed by
the demanding life of a blackman
who could make millions
for a white record company...

THIS GREAT BLACK MAN
AS MILLIONS OF PEOPLE WALKED INSIDE HIS SOUL
and his hands,
touched my eyes so softly

The smashing beat of his form
The form of Macon,
The form and soul
of the Black Man creating light
The engulfing rhythm of his voice
closing out the pain, making the
Sadness in Sayeeda cry out: "IT'S TRUE"
"IT'S TURE!! O, GOD IT'S TRUE!!!"
singing his sad, sad song
singing his sad, sad song

THE LOVE this man had
was a love handed All Black people
from the deep black earth
from the days of our freedom
from the days of our nations
from the women's thighs, weighed down with child
from the silent, old men, sittin' in southern rockers
from the Red, Black, and Green awaiting our lost people

Cries as Malcolm,
Cries as Malcolm,
RESPECT!!!
RESPECT!!!
RESPECT!!!
AND A CHANGE IS GONNA COME
AND A CHANGE IS GONNA COME
SING IT OTIS
SING IT OTIS
RESPECT
RESPECT
RESPECT
AND A CHANGE IS GONNA COME...

gaston neal feb. 4, 1968

JUST INTONATION AND THE NEW BLACK REVOLUTIONARY MUSIC

In an innocuous essay published in a nation-wide bi-weekly Jazz magazine a white musician-critic undertook an analysis of the music of Ornette Coleman. In the course of the analysis he stated that since Ornette's variable-pitch notes occurred generally on steps of the diatonic scale other than the octave or the fifth that this indicated a tonal conception closer to "just", than "tempered" intonation.

This may seem meaningless to many laylisteners, non-musicians and musicians alike, but it touches significantly on a very essential aspect of Black music; the pitch-components of the music, the "noise" elements utilized by the new Black music.

When melodic instruments began to complement the human voice, to a great extent they were all alike, they all shared a crude similarity. Thus there were little differentiation of the kinds of pitches one culture produced as against another. These sounds were produced without or very little regard of systematic relationships. The musicians of these different cultures also began to notice and enjoy intervals of varying sizes, from the smallest the ear could recognize to the largest the voice or instrument could produce.

In the systemization that inevitably followed, that inevitably developed musicians of all of these cultures discarded sounds which proved hopelessly irregular, but most of them kept the smaller tones, the quarters and thirds. Western European music did, in its development, eliminate these smaller intervals and in doing so erected a distinctive harmonic structure, a vertical relationship of tones. At the expense of sacrificing, for the sake of harmonic and tonal regularity a vast field of musical possibilities a Western musical system was devised.

It is this vast area of musical possibilities that Jazz music has always explored because Jazz music is a product of Black people. And the music of Black peoples must be considered in context to their distinctive culture, not as an entirely Western development as that development is understood as an white European development, but as a development of a non-white people, a non-white culture which applies and agrees completely with the musical development we cited above.

Even after such long exposure to Western music we are still essentially Eastern people. The distinctive timbre, the treatment of pitch, distinctive features of all Black music - though it can be attributed to the Black aesthetic in a general sense - can also be seen as the ebullience of the Black musical genius.

In 1928, a Dr. Milton Metfessel observed in black folksingers, especially blues singers a constant habit of hitting a note that did not appear in the equal-tempered musical scale.

This note he called a "neutral third" because though it appeared between the tonic and the 3rd, it was a little less than 5 vibrations-a-second lower in pitch than the third in the equal-tempered scale. It suggested a flatted or minor third. But actually this "neutral third" was seldom sung by itself of precisely "in tune". Actually what the doctor had located was the aggregate pitch of the notes in this area. Hithertofore many "learned" white musical "authorities" and their black counterpart dismissed this as a childish blunder characteristic of a childish development. However in Dr. Metfessel's pioneer work[1] he was forced to conclude that it was intentional and fundamental to black music. This brought him and others to the logical conclusion "that this consistent gravitation toward a neutral 3rd is due to a feeling for a non-European scale - a scale other than the equal-tempered scale .... presumably a scale which is found in Africa."[2]

And now ... just what is the relationship of all of this to "just" intonation and the new revolutionary music?

Initially "just" intonation had no particular meaning to me. But quite by accident while perusing a manual on piano tuning I discovered the meaning and distinction between "just" and "tempered" intonation.

Each tone on the keyboard is regularly tuned by counting the number of vibrations that constitute that tone. These vibrations determine the characteristic of the tone. They establish a tone as a "c", as a "d", as a "e" and so forth. This means that the 12 pitches of the piano are spaced intervallically by a seemingly logical and orderly progression of vibrations. Yet we find that if we were to tune the piano, within the span of an octave, in this manner, starting with middle "c" that when we reach it's octave ("c" twelve pitches or tones away) it will be "out of tune" in respect to the initial middle "c", This is an essentially elementary explanation of "just" tuning. Yet in this small and limited explanation it is extremely apparent why the tones in the Western musical contruct cannot ever be accurately determined as the western tonal system implies. It demonstanes the natural inconsistencies of musical pitches, of what exist as natural and of what exist as entirely manmade, of what is orderly and agreeable (which is merely a cultural convenience) which boils down to mean what is agreeable to what people, what is agreeable to what culture? What is agreeable to white culture? What is agreeable to Black culture?

1- Dr. Milton Metfessel, a white musicologist and acoustician who wrote a pioneering book in this area, PHONOPHOTOGRAPHY IN FOLK MUSIC (Chapel Hill; University of North Carolina Press)

2- Marshall Stearns, STORY OF JAZZ (Oxford University Press, 1956)

One is related to one culture and the other is related to the other culture. This is why any critique on the music must entail its culture. Not American culture because that implies the American white culture, but the American Black culture. Thus the frame of reference in any critique on Black music must invoke criterias of all non-white people, criterias on the music of Black people in Africa, the people of Asia, of China and India. When the white musicologist speaks about the introduction of the "blues" pitch or tone into the western musical complex he is speaking about the aesthetic evocation of a non-white people, a stylized equivalent of a distinctive tonal orientation, entirely different to his own. So aside from whatever conclusion he might arrive at as a self appointed arbiter of our music, he nonetheless illustrates the inadequacy of the Western diatonic musical system to express the Black experience.

Now Black music vis a vis the white musical tradition has always been revolutionary. Stated another way, within the white cultural ethos the music of the oppressed Black people has always been "disrespectful" and the residual remains of such an attitude persist today in the recondite articles that one encounters in Jazz periodicals. This, I am very happy to observe, is indulged in by white intellectuals primarily, and being white, they base their evaluation of the art on their own white cultural premises.

We reject, more emphatically then our predessors, most of the Western white musical criterias. Our music has always rejected the established musical norm of the West. Though never to the extent it is rejected today in the music of Milford Graves for instance, or Giuseppi Logan. Or Sonny Murray. We are challenging, more than ever before the entire musical construction of the Western world. Where formally we were contented to work through it which to a certain historical extent is why in America there exist that amalgam of Black and white musics: Jazz, we chose to emphasize factors of our aesthetic in the sole knowledge of its validity as a distinct cultural entity.

We now seem more compelled to work out from our own Black aesthetic. This distinguishes us from the Bebop develcoment which successfully accomplished what it set out to achieve, eg., to accommodate aesthetically the restrictions of a white harmonic system to the aesthetic configurations of distend culture, the Black culture in America. This it achieved by extending, by an elaborate use of western musical material and an audacious array of permuted elements (the likes of which have never been seen in any of the artforms of the West) the harmonic vocabulary of the music, which was still (and to some extent still is) rooted in a popular song formal and harmonically moored.

This is why the work of Ornette Coleman epitomizes the solution of essentially distend musical aggregates, Ornette epitomizes solutions that distinctly declare they do not abide nor accommmodate an essentially alien musical tradition. This is what made the music of Ornette Coleman revolutionary. This is why the music of the Fifties, though innovationally revolutionary (which explains why the movement then, was typified by an extreme technical expansiveness) was not revolutionary in the sense the new Black music is. The Bebop phase did not challenge the established musical form. It introduced configurations, that successfully superseded the older conventions. It was merely the strangeness of this new arrangement that brought so much opposition to the music of Bird and Monk. The form remained intact. But the challenge we present is toward the much larger Western musical hegemony. The entire musical edifice the white Western world has erected and founded its music on.

This is why I believe that an understanding of the "just" condition in music could serve as a fulcrum with which the Black individual could extricate himself from the sticture s of a musical system which is the product of an alien white culture.

Seen in perspective Bird was largely an aesthetic accommodationist. In terms of the vast contribution he made to the music his compositional output was almost infinitesimal. This would seem to indicate that Bird's genius resided in the superimposition of his unique methodology on a tired and depleted tradition eg. the jazz of the Thirties.

Most of, all of Bird's music conformed to the lyric-ballad form. His entire creative output was presented within the frame of this lyric-form and in the ubiquitous blues form. The 12 measure blues form. Antecedents for these two forms can be found in the early English ballad form, and in the early madrigals and other folk forms of the white European cultures.

The blues form like all of our musics in the West is a mixture. The over-all length and proportions is European-derived but the inner form is African.

It's interesting to note that the 12 measure form that we have come to associate with the blues form is a fairly recent development. The earlier forms of the blues were radically different from the present form. They were essentially more "African", complying as they did to the "call and response" pattern - perculier to African song-forms - which provided a more varied frame of more infinitely complicated components.

To the extent that this essay will be invariably read by some white person and being aware at the same time that it is intended to be read by my Black brothers and sisters, I know and I am fully cognizant of the fact that the reader of this paper brings with him or her, like the playgoer preconditioned ideas about the catagory of music in the Western experience. And to that extent they are preconditioned to what they will call music in their shared Western experience. Which means we must encounter resistence from our Black brother as well as we invariably will from the whites. Our brother is our concern. It is him we are concerned about. Not whites. So it is to him and her that this paper is humbly submitted.

Writing is an educated activity and like it or not it is indulged by educated people. But educated people are often intellectually stereotypal, they indulge in intellectual miscreants as deviously reprehensive as those of the illiterate. Which means that the music or the paper thus submitted may be no less accessible to the black person that reads it, then to the white person that reads it. By and large the intellectual apprehension of musical experience has been a largely white endeavor and the persons, black or white that enjoin this kind of intellectual procedure are, to a greater or lesser degree involved in the pursuit, or inquiry of, an activity that the mass of Black people have neither the time or the patience for.

And all the time the Black individual who might read this essay is programmed to a white musical criteria. Thus I have no doubts that the music would be just as incongruous to his organization of what is music and what is not. And inasmuch as aesthetic standards are not inborn but acquired, the point of this paper is to attempt a delineation of a specific noumenal situation. The delineation of a noumenal situation that is agreeable with the compost of the Black culture.

Addenda

In the historical continuum of Western European music we will now, for the educated reader establish contemporary music.

We must begin by saying that in the development of Western music Pythagoras must be blamed for discrepancies that occurred in the evolution of the western musical system. In his attempt to standardize the arts he restricted the tonal scale to seven pitches so that they comply with the seven basic colors of the western color system. In his attempt to standardize an almost infinite variety of aural differentiations he arbitrarily established a false system. He established a fixed tonal system, that though it must be credited for facilitating an elaborate and complex harmonic system, it nevertheless precluded the infinite tonal richness, subtlety and variety that those other finer aspects of the tonal spectrum could have enhanced it. These finer tonal elements were retained by the non-white cultures in their music. This is what the Western white musical tradition is encountering in the music of the Black people in the West. This is what the musical tradition encountered in the spirtuals. This is what the white musical tradition encountered in the blues. And this is what the white musical tradition is encountering in the new Black revolutionary music.

James T. Stewart

THE NEW BLACK MUSIC

by James T. Stewart

Our music must bring down the white empire.
We come down on them like marauders breathing
black chrysalis of sounds smashing their cellos,
climbing down from the walls
to perform execution on all
tempered music teachers in
iron-eyed do - ra - mes
ramming terrible beauty to their minds
knocking plugs from their ears.
We must run through concert halls
knocking over seats and set fire to programs,
dance on the laps of white mink myopic bitches
and yoke all faggot music lovers,
psalmist, pink ladies
and sell insurances to b'nith beth
mumbling liberals in their underwear.
Mean black mamas turning white anglo-saxon
storekeepers into zombies
while police in leotards bite caps off of beer cans.

Further Comment On The Empty Foxhole

Ornette's album exposed Shelley Manne for the sham I always thought he was. Quoting this jive honky drummer: "That is unadulterated s.... (Shelly Manne's spelling). It sounds like I was standing in the middle of some kids rehearsal hall and all these people were playing in different rooms." These are Manne's opening remarks in the November 2, 1967 issue of Downbeat magazine. Commenting on Denardo Coleman's drumming (Denardo is Orenette's 10 yr old son), Manne says: "As a drummer that kid will probably turn out to be a good carpenter, I mean if that's the way he's starting out."

There we have it a put-down of the record and Ornette's son. These remarks again put out the gap between the Afro-American creative artist and the white critic. Be the critic a "musician" or not.

Denardo Coleman's playing on this album is fresh and pregnant with surprise. Unlike Shelly Manne, Denardo's conception of time and rhythm has not been ordered and forced into a European framework. Consequently, Ornette is able to feel a greater sense of freedom; the pieces are not shaped by the usual technical considerations. We make or create time instead of keeping time like a metronome. "To keep" time is a Western concept which almost means boxing in time. If you want that kind of "order" then keep right on listening to drummers like Shelly Manne. But if you want a more expanded universe, a multi-sided, concept of time check out drummers like Milford Graves, Rashid Ali, Beaver Harris, and a whole lot of good young men. But back to the Empty Foxhole, Ornette's approach to this whole thing is honest. If he is looking for relatively new patterns, it is perfectly consistent to have his 10 yr old son on this date. The patterns would be fresh and startling, and there would almost naturally be an absence of cliches. And this is precisely the results.

Finally, Shelly Manne is probably fucked up over this side because he lacked an equivalent amount of creativity when he was 10 yrs old. Frankly, Denardo's play is even now more interesting than anything Manne's got to say. Especially, since he is a poor imitation of Max Roach who probably taught the honky everything he knows.

All of this is not to invest any particular musical genius in Ornette's son. But rather, it is to assert a kind of naturalness absent in more self-conscious musicians. Further Denardo's very "ineptness" and "awkardness" are an interesting contrast to the folk elements inherent in Ornette's playing.

L. N.

CRICKET needs money. You received a free one. Won't you contribute money for materials and postage? $1.00 a year makes you a CRICKETEER. Less than that is still cool tho. Don't misunderstand. Most CRICKETS are given away free. But to a small percentage of our readers, like you, we feel we can ask for some dough!

Thank

CRICKETS

JIHAD (PUBLISHERS OF THE CRICKET)

Books MUSIC ART Plays FILM Drama

ALL ABOUT BLACK PEOPLE

BOOKS

AFRO-ARTS ANTHOLOGY .... New work by Larry Neal, Q. R. Hand, Ben Caldwell, Le Roi Jones, Yusef Iman, David Henderson, Sonia Sanchez, Joseph White, Ed Spriggs, annonymous yellers $1.00

BLACK ART .... New Poems by Le Roi Jones $1.00

NOT FOREVER TEARS .... Poems by Clarence Reed $1.00

SLAVE SHIP .... A one-act.play by Le Roi Jones $1.25

BLACK WOMAN'S ROLE IN THE REVOLUTION! .... A much needed re-defining of why and how the "Queen of the World" must function NOW, and in the coming Struggle. A MUST for every BLACK FAMILY $1.25

ARM Yourself OR HARM Yourself! .... A play by Le Roi Jones $1.00

MILITANT PREACHER .... One Act Play by Ben Caldwell $1.00

PRAISE THE LORD, BUT PASS THE AMMUNITION .... A play by Yusef Iman $1.00

SOMETHING BLACK .... Poems by Yusef Iman $1.00

BLACK REVOLUTIONARY SONGS .... by Yusef Iman $1.00

FILMS

BLACK SPRING .... A documentary of the BLACK ARTS alliance travels on the West Coast, Spring 1967. Features: Stokely Carmichael, H. Rap Brown, Huey P. Newton, Le Roi Jones, Floyd McKissick Rental Fee $50.00

DUTCHMAN .... A film based on the award winning play by Le Roi Jones Rental Fee $100.00

RECORDS

BLACK and BEAUTIFUL! .... Soul Music Full of Black Power and Genius. Yusef Iman, The JIHAD Singers, Le Roi Jones, reading 33LP $5.00

About the beauty of black women 45 disc $1.00

SONNY'S TIME NOW! .... Sonny Murray, drums; Albert Ayler, tenor; Don Cherry, trumpet; Henry Grimes, bass; Louis Worrell, bass; Le Roi Jones, reading, "Black Art" 33LP $5.00

DRAMA

SPIRIT HOUSE PLAYERS AND MOVERS
The Black Repertory Theater
The Living Word!

We'll bring B L A C K A R T to you! Anywhere in the country!

FOR FURTHER INFORMATION WRITE:

JIHAD Productions
P. O. Box 663
Newark, New Jersey

Recent productions: We Own the Night .. by Jimmy Garrett
Great Goodness of Life .. by Le Roi Jones

Issue 3
(1968)

73–110

THE CRICKET

CONTENTS PAGE

THE CRICKET

Black Music In Evolution

Editors: LeRoi Jones, Larry Neal, A.B. Spellman

Advisors: Sun Ra, Milford Graves, Cecil Taylor

Correspondents: Gaston Neal, Wash, DC, Stanley Crouch, LA; James Stewart, Philadelphia, Clyde Halisi, LA; Don L. Lee, Chicago, Norman Jordan, Cleveland, Ben Caldwell, New York, Larry Miller, New Ark, more to come

ORDER OF ARTICLES — PAGE

LETTER FROM ATLANTA

I've been out of the City for four months now and I don't miss it much. The war there is too grey, too general; the targets too hard to fix your sights on, except where they're uniformed like at the rent office. The devils there vamp you. Some folks keep them out of their living rooms o.k. but they will be on the Subways, in the audience, or at the bookstores, or on the other side of the dollar, telling you how like Che Guevara, who was white, they are. The machine gun in the head gets rusty, its firing pin wears down after you've offed your first thousand or so for the day. The nice guy game that commerce makes you play gets in you and you play it by rote until you are it. The world then becomes two or three billion individuals and you start clearing spaces in your head for the 'fays who want to come over to your side until the WHO I AM that you cultivated so carefully to keep you straight becomes WHO AM I? with a question mark about 5' 11½" tall and weighing about 215 pounds. I guess there are some brothers who don't go through those changes at all and some who do but don't sweat it, and some others who fight it so hard their tubes blow out.

Here the air is much cleaner. I go days and days and see no greys, and the ones I see carry some idicia, like those portable files the bill collectors carry, tho a surprisingly large number of ofays come sniffing after black genitals in the large Negro night clubs. But "individuals" come individually, and not in human wave suicide squads. Black power, black consciousness is not camp here, except sometimes with students. When the grassroots people say they dig it, they dig it - no bullshit about it. And when they don't dig it they tell you to kiss their ass. And when they say they don't know it means they really don't know, and the questions they ask are worth asking. The Movement people, particularly the SNCC folk, have paid their dues and continue to do so without wearing a DIG MY DUES button. The Minister at the Mosque, a very down and accessible brother named John Shabazz, has a good political head, can rap, and doesn't comfort himself as if his porkless shit doens't stink. There are several good minds in Atlanta, and enough together people passing through that I don't feel cut off from what's happening on the coast and in Detroit and Chicago and in The City. The pace is slower, but moving.

So what's there to miss in New York? Friends, yes, but otherwise I'll sign the City over to the first trick who wants it, except for the music and that's a drag. Charles Lloyd, who I do not dig, was here a month ago and I went to see him twice. Two weeks before, I almost went to see Ramsey Lewis. WHERE'S THE GODDAMN MUSIC? Ormaybe I should ask, why is the music?

Here, there is nothing that's worth relating, musically. You can see Rev. Pearly Brown at the same coffeehouse that showed Lyn Chandler, but why dig Pearly Brown in a white coffee house? Why dig anybody there.

This is the hole contemporary black "jazz" musicians are struggling with. Why can't a man who wants to play work in Atlanta or Birmingham in a context that makes his music work for something? There are some cats who play their horns well, but what comes out is of the 'fifties, of Benny Golson, Horace Silver, etc. and, at best, of the Monk revival. Straight No Chaser is as far out as they'll go. There are piano players here who say they've come to terms with McCoy Tyner, but I've yet to hear Cecilj Taylor's name mentioned by anybody.

But even still, the cats have a hard time making it. You think jazz gigs are tight in the Apple? In Atlanta they want a flavor of jazz, no more. The clubs are mostly for the bougies, and their taste is worst than the devils'. Paschal's Carousel, the steadiest gig in town, has had a 2/3rds hunkie trio which plays inept watered down Bill Evans. Flush it. There's a brother with a record store on Hunter Street who knows what's happening, but I think he'd order about three of the Trane, Om, probably one of a new Shepp, a couple of Jackie's, no Sun Ra.

I'm trying to draw a death picture of the New Music among black folk in Atlanta. It is not much different in Harlem, not that much. Or Decatur, or Southwest Georgia. Harlem musicians still make it downtown to blow and be blown. I met a good brother in Birmingham who plays tenor, loves his people, loves his horn, wants to blow. He has a thing for Sun Ra and is going crazy in the soul gigs he has to take in Birmingham to get his coins together to get out of town to study with the master. I have never heard him, but I'd be surprised if he ain't a bitch. He hates the devil, but that big pink cock of a Lower East Side is pulling at him like the tide, deathward, toward the corruption, competition with his brothers, drugs, and worse, a successful market of white people. Unless some rapport is established uptown.

I'm told of pockets of the Music in most of the large cities of America, particularly in Detroit, Chicago, etc. and they say there's a lot in San Francisco. But the audience is probably 2/3 white, and the cats hung up in rationalizations about when they're going to take it home. People say, it didn't take that long for Bird and Monk and Miles and them to catch on with the black community, why should these cats be so out of it if they're really into something? Wellllll, I really can't say for sure, but I'm going to throw some things out and leave the question open. For one thing, Bird and them changed the scene, absolutely, and I don't just mean in a musicological sense. They created like Yakub the magician, the hip white boy. They created the idea of hip, a whole life style the white people copied off us. Somehow, a neutral turf grew around this - I think because the Music of the 'forties was definitely small band, club music, you might say chamber. Black bands before would play dances in both black and white neighborhoods, but then the whiteys would be trying to imitate our dances and not our lives, and the musicians could commute. But the white entrepreneur dug the hip white audience, and put the music in midtown in the heart of the showbiz world, and when the fickle white hipsters starte d digging whatever it was they started digging after Bird, enough years had elapsed for the Music to be alienated, and there was nowhere it could lay but Bohemia. Another major factor is the refusal of the mass communications media to project the Music in a time when these media greatly shaped tastes and ideas. So Harlem heard little of the Music for over 20 years.

Now there are a hundred things wrong with this theory, and I'm naming trends, not laws. First, white people have always imitated some of what they thought was black life style, particularly in the 'twenties and themselves when they "slummed" to Duke Ellington. But I don't believe they listened as hungrily for, say the latest black vernacular as they did in the 'forties. Second, there were several big bands in Bird's time, and they were always concerts, like at the Apollo and dances played by small and large bands. But it's also true that this was the period of the decline of the ballroom and the big band . Why not? He, K. C. Bird, was a band by himself. I'm not so sure what happened to the uptown bar scene and the jam session. I'm not from New York originally, and I didn't live through it. It sounds too simple to say that 52nd st. just drained Harlem dry, but it seems that's what happened.

But since I moved to the Village in '59 and stayed for eight years, I saw quite a few changes go down on that end. The Open Door had closed before I came up but the Bohemia thrived for a minute, right around the corner from Cafe Society, where Christine Jorgenson had a strip act, if you can get to that. The Village Vanguard was and is prosperous, and the Half Note, though they hire white and near white musicians for the most part. Then the Terminis struck gold on the Bowery with Cecil Taylor and, later, Monk. They had the Five Spot and the Jazz Gallery, both of which catered to the hop, making it, white bohemian art set. Then that big barn of a club, the Village Gate. Now they're Slug's, and there've been a number of passing fancies in between.

What's missing in all this is black owners and black audiences, and ways out of the barroom. Black music has never lost it's whorehouse connotation and never will as long as white people are the main body of the paying audience, which I think has always been the case for the Music. And if we ever find a way of bringing it back home to the black community, which is easily the most pressing problem the music faces, then it must have some function other than selling drinks. In the bars listed above, black people were neither welcome nor comfortable. Nor was serious black music truly welcome or comfortable, as the length and intensity of the music interfered with commerce. The tourist element was a larger determinant of the choice of musicians than the nature of the music and the whole scene was altogether unnatural. For a minute we thought loft parties would pick up the slack, but they never really paid off and practically the only brothers who came had tremendous hardons that throbbed so hard after white pussy that all other purpose was negated.

It was a sick scene and got sicker as the Lower East Side opened up. Unlike the village, black people were in on the recent settling of the East Side. It was predominantly Jewish before, with some Italian, Polish, Ukranian and god knows what else. Black folk pushed in from the projects on the East River, others migrated in from Brooklyn and Harlem, but there was a world of difference between the newcomers in the projects and the hip ones from uptown. They never did get together in any meaningful way. Our oyez brothers are the strongest group on the East Side, and how they make it with the growing black settlement will determine the social development of the East Side against the incursion of the hippies with their portable heat.

With the possible exception of some enclaves in Brooklyn, I don't believe there are so many black musicians in residence anywhere in this hemisphere. To name a few, Sun Ra,

Marion Brown (now in Europe), Archie Shepp, Pharoah Saunders, Jackie McLean, Cecil Taylor, Sunny Mūrray and many, many others are based there, though it is in the nature of black musicians to be perambulatory.

Gigs are tight and usually set at scale wage. There are dogfights for the few gigs that exist that are embarrassing and repulsive when you think that the Black Musicians' need for self organization is at least as pressing as that of other segment of the black community. It gets so that one musician won't say anything good about another musician. Everybody says everybody else is stealing their shit. A lot of brothers drink too much wine and use too much dope. There's nothing I can think of to recommend the East Side for black musicians or any other black artists, except that the concentration is so great that it's a good place to learn from your contemporaries. Otherwise flush it, I've seen too many good brothers go there and die. It's like moving into a plague.

Still they all go to the lower East Side, or almost all. Some go home, like Milford Graves and Robin Kenyatta and Andrew Hill and you can hear their music growing for that reason: they play most often in the Black community, in sets designed to put black culture in its proper perspective: as the esthetic vanguard of the struggle. This means that the chance to get rich is abdicated, but there is a concommittant thickness to this Music that is missing in much of the New Music, a thickness of African identity that is felt and not forced. It is that identity that feeds Sun Ra's music, and made John Coltrane the scream of all of us. Many of us wanted the musicians to go "out" but didn't mean for them to take their roots with them. Black music is and always has been essentially a call (to action) and an answer (a movement), and audience feedback, even if it's a hunkie audience, is bound to affect the music. For one thing, there is too much art for art's sake bourgeois individualism, anathema to the community concept of today's black vanguard. Most often, no specific programmatic political interpretation can be attached to the Music, but the uses to which the Musicians put the Music is an adequate determinant.

It is understandable that the Musicians should be waiting for a liberator who would put together new record companies, community based music rooms, black publishing companies, etc., but it just ain't happening. They've got to do it for themselves. This magazine sould be produced, edited and written by musicians. The Jazz Composer's Guild should have been all black and should have held together.

And all musicians shouldn't be from Atlanta.

These are my thoughts as I wait for records to come in the mail. Where's the goddamn music? Why does it seek out a death audience? Who loves the Music? Who does the Music love?

Memorial

1. The supremes - cuz they dead

the supremes done gone
and sold their soul
to tar
zan and other
honkey / raper.
They sing rogers
and hart songs
as if we didn't
have enough andrew
sisters spitting their
whiter than mr.
clean songs in our faces.
YEAH.
the supremes
done gone
and bleached out
their blk / ness
and all that is heard
is
me. tarzan
u. jane
and
bwana.
bwana.
bwana.

Sonia Sanchez

"SUN RA"

Sun Ra showed me his world tonight, he gave actual proof to the existence of a living sound dimension And Beyond.

Sun Ra created an energy music mass, a mass of music that moves the mind to a point million years past timelessness, or spacelessness.

Everything in the room was electrified, even when the Arkestra stopped playing their voices were charged with an electric force that projected through all the physical bodies present.

I knew that Sun Ra, had the Power to blast us all off the Planet, our every being, was in his hands as they like meteors jeted across, his cosmic keyboard, faster than your realization of them.

Sun Ra, is the Son of Ra, he defies all descriptions, one can only see Sun Ra, hear Sun Ra, and try to describe Sun Ra,
he being not of this world, defies all earthly adjectives, nouns, or pronouns, he is a cosmic character, controller of a time we have not reached yet.

In his music, we are allowed to see previews of another time, another place, a unbelievable extension of the Black psyche.

Sun Ra is a lower of the forces of tomorrow, his music is love as a pure emotion, love that can exist within your mind for the single reason of making you realize what it is, it does not have to be channelled to a human party, it is past the human releases and expressions of its' being, it is a love that thrives in the heart to guide the thoughts towards higher Stratas of Soul, or maybe even Solar Soul.

Sun Ra's eyes are the electrified eyes of Egypt, gleeming through the sound mass of musical sunshine.

Ra has lived in every period of time since time was created, probably out of the mind of a Blackman, he has advanced through all the periods of time and gone on ahead to prepare a place for the Blackman in the Outer Limits of a more POWERFUL EXISTENCE.

Clyde Halisi

blackmusic/a beginning

pharoah sanders
had
finished
playing
&
the whi
te boy [illegible] was to
go on next.

him didn't

him sd
that
his horn
was
broke.

they sat
there
dressed in
african garb
& dark sun glasses
listening to the brothers
play. (taking notes)
we
didn't realize
who they
were un
til their
next recording
had been
released: the beach boys play soulmusic.

real sorry about
the supremes
being dead,
heard some whi
te girls
the other day---
all wiged down
with a mean tan---
sounden just like them,
singen
rodgers & hart
& some country & western.

don l. lee

POSITION PAPER

(Presented at the Black Aesthetic & Black Artist workshop conducted by LeRoi Jones and Milford Graves at the 3rd International Conference on Black Power which convened in Philadelphia August 29 to September 1st)

REVOLUTIONARY BLACK MUSIC IN THE TOTAL CONTEXT OF BLACK DISTENSION

Black music in the total context of our Black thrust must stimulate and energize our Black aesthetic vision. We must promulgate the principles of our Black creations. We must prepare our people through our art.

Because music proceeds as movement and force music is the ultimate aesthetic equivalent of revolutionary Black thought. Music is process in motion and it is the best paradigm of the nature and movement of reality we have to teach us, why we must change reality. And because all art supports and substantiates the values of its people, nationalism, the ideological redact of our culture validates our art. Our music. Because, not unless our art/music is qualified by the cultural imperatives of a philosophy that emanates from the basic idea of our Black nationhood, our art/music is a distortion. It will be like the existing mainstream jazz situation today running in the same white economic rut controlled and manipulated by the beast. Plantation style. Black music accompanies those Black brothers and sisters whose aim and philosophy is the destruction of whitemind culture that obfuseates and pollutes the only, the most viable dynamic capable of sustaining our culture: our nationhood. Black music is the ritualized performance of what we are, what we are being and what we will be.

Check it out. White art is what everything was. Never what something is.

We must know, unequivocally and understand the objectives of Black music/art, revolutionary Black/art music in terms of revolution. Black art/music is the aesthetic equivalent of Black revolution in our minds evolving and creating our nation. We are involved in the erection of our own aesthetic edifice. On the conviction that all art proceeds from program and a set of values which spring from its cultural grid, which in turn determines the critique and finally solidifies the creative residuem - we have an authentic art/product - the new Blk/art music for new Black people. And this is why the music we speak of, we call revolutionary. We reject entirely, a white musical system.

We reject entirely the basic foundations of the white western tempered musical system and proceed instead from the aesthetic ground of our own Black culture. Art for Black people is the art Blk people created. That art has always been Black. Out of a Black matrix. Not white death/art. Living Black art with Black nomenclatures. Black art is movement, being and becoming. Black art is fluid. Black creation is flux. Speech, poetry, dance and music. The question as to whether a critique is needed is a white intellectual question, which itself precludes the intrinsic criterias of the Black creative context.

Creators do not ask questions of the process of creation. They create as momentary tracers of the flow of being, or as attuners participate in the flow, accentuating the operation of being.

Nothing needs to be "read," into what is created. Creation, in essence is what is becoming. Creation is involved in change. You cannot create without changing. Something comes to be, to exist that never came to be or existed before. But creation is more than merely change. It is progression and process and in the ritualized act - the art act - the only art man can make is the "act" art (the way Black people do) in the arts that change, the arts that move. These are the life arts, living. The art of Black people. Changing. Duking reality. Sliding slick white mummies to their masters in museums.

Revolutionary creation refers to the context, our Black world context wherein what is being created also prepares those people, our Black people now in the present for the context of the world to come in our Black nationhood. By this reason and expressly for this purpose our new Black music must be understood in terms of an aesthetic erection in the context of the Third World which we are issuing in.

We cannot be readied for this order of existence, this order of our culture snapping our fingers in bars, befogging our minds with liquor, gibbering to white gods. We must smash all white musical criterias, releasing our force as our force is released by our Black spirit. Black music must assail white western musical organization.

Black music is guerrilla music. Terrorist music. Revolutionary music. Everytime we stand before the world we confront and attack all the established norms of the organization of music, white music. There, you see how the revolutionary rhetoric agrees with and approximates the properties of music. This is one of the ways music teaches. This is one of the ways music must teach us in our Black revolutionary contest.

Black music is the accompaniment of the vision of the Black nation we are bringing to reality, with Blk poets and singers and playwrites constructing new Black poetry and musics for the Black nation.

We are erecting national theatres. Revolutionary theatres bivouacing in the wilderness of the white empire cities. Portable theatres. Spirit House. NEW SCHOOL OF AFRO-AMERICAN THOUGHT. Black music activating Blk minds in white colleges. Preparation US

We are psalmist to Obatala, the Yoruba Gode of creation. Creating new tonalities. New instruments. Black instrumentation.

We are musicians, poets working out of a basic and fundamental truth that our art is conceived in terms of whom it is conceived for, and what kind of order the world will be in, for it to be in.

Not only art but everything else, once it comes, in a correct analysis a Black analysis of our reality will proceed from these fundamental premises. Black power proceeds from this black analysis of the state of being of Blk people in America.

ADDENDA

All valid art springs from an ideological base. A system of values. And our artists expresses these values if they are artists of any substance. Not as autonomous individuals as a few of our brothers appear to be. Attractive as they may seem. But men possessing a program A conception of the world in terms of a system of values posited in the corporate consciousness of our people. In our instance, the consciousness of our black collectivity.

Finally, those dedicated to change, to new concepts, political and aesthetic must be relentless and persistent. We must be ruthless, because we know that those who are contented, the believers in the status quo, the established order of things will not voluntarily give up their ideas on the organization of things. Change never comes about in an orderly fashion. It will not be achieved by the rational agreement of the oppressed people and the oppressor, meeting and discussing Those dedicated to change, revolutionaries, must dismantle the economic, political and cultural relationships in the white capitalist society which are based on the imposition of one man and his society on another.

We cannot cajcle change. We must destroy the whitemind music in the mind of Blk people today.

Change is always in the present toward the future, so that all of the immediate past - the tradition and all its restraints in what is called "things as they are" the "established way of doing things" MUST BE DESTROYED.

In this sense, there is absolutely no continuous link between the way things were and the way things are at the moment, or the way things will be. Not as conscious history. The revolutionary must destroy the prison the present makes of dreams.

On developing a black cultural movement, we must define what is Black Art. To define what the technical aspects of Black Art are, we must first develope a black feeling. To develope a black feeling we must work and live, within the black community to understand the problems of black people. After developing a feeling we must have black institutions, that will make Black Art a practical reality. Institutions that will provide the Black Artist with grants, scholarships, & fellowships. Institutions to train the artist and people and at the same time will provide for creative workshops.

Because we have lacked a strong economic program for Black Artist in the past, the Black Artist has strongly depended on the white western oppressive system for economic help. Black people must realize that the system has greatly benefited from Black Art on an economic basis. We must realize that the art of Black Music alone if controlled by black people will provide the balck people with economic power that only the white oppressor has enjoyed. We are the creators of Rhythm & Blues, Jazz, and The New Black Revolutionary Music, we are the raw material that the white oppressor has used to strengthen his survival and weaken ours.

We must realize that a strong economic program that is controlled by black people will keep the Black Artist in the community, it will give the Black Artist a sense of security, it will stop the Black Artist from thinking that by using White-Western musical theory he will be guaranteed a musical survival. We must realize that self-help programs is our only way. When we have strong black controlled economic programs we will have a strong Black Art.

We must have black self-help programs that will function on a collective basis. Black Music must be a black peoples music, it must be a flexible music, a music that reflexes the objective reality of black people. Black Music must understand the principles of African Music, that Black Music must be for communicative purposes and not for abstractness. We must realize that Black Music is one of the best weapons for organizing black people, we must not waste time when black people attend Black Music affairs by using a music that is composed of Western elements. Any music that has elements from the enemy is of no use to black people.

We must have black music literature like LeRoi Jones' BLACK MUSIC, and THE CRICKET magazine, to uplift the morale of the black musicians, books, magazines, leaflets, etc. that will guide black musicians & people in a positive direction.

We need self-help recording companies to be operated on a collective basis. If we don't have black recording programs the black musician will depend on white-owned companies that will only exploit his genius to record his work. This will suppress black musical creativity because the black musician will have to compromise by doing what the enemy dictates to him, i. e. he will tell you to utilize Western theory. Western theory is the product of the very person who enslaved us.

We need new instruments, instruments that will be more related to balck expression, these instruments will be beneficial on the economic level. Black people have been the greatest non-paid advertising agents for the major instrument makers. When one black musician asks another respected black musican what kind of instrument he plays, his answer should not be one such as a selma saxaphone (selma is a white owned instrument maker) but one that is a product of a black controlled instrument factory.

We must call a Black Artist Conference to talk about subjects such as the coordination of all the Black Arts (Art, Music, Dance, Poetry, Drama, etc.) We need a black national orchestra. This orchestra will be a great weapon to bring about a United

Musician front. Black Music must be the product of black life which will be expressed by a national black orchestra.

Milford Graves

OLIVER NELSON — Live From Los Angeles — Impulse A9153

I heard this once each side. It's bullshit. And hard to take, but this has been on up at us, coming down the line, for awhile now. Oliver has been selling his ass for days. Now the manifestation seems final, and ugly.

Does anybody remember his Screamin The Blues with Eric Dolphy? At that time Oliver was a motherfucker on his instrument too. Check him out, what he was doing. He aint doing nothing, now. He aint into nothing, but bullshit. Dont check this side out. It sucks.

(You remember Blues & The Abstract Truth, then? OK, well, he done left all that way behind ..... like nothing, really.

Music the Neglected Plane of Wisdom

Music is a plane of wisdom, because music is a
universal language. It is a language of honor, it
is a noble precept, a gift of the Airy Kingdom.
Music is air, a universal existence . . . common
to all the living.

Music is existence, the key to the universal
language,

Because it is the universal language ....
Freedom of Speech is Freedom of Music.
Music is not material. Music is spiritual.
Music is a living soul force.
That which is of the soul is the greater light
The light of greater instruction ...
The light of culture and beauty,
The light of intensity of living power.
The name of Music is Art.
The name is Music played by infinite instruments.
The name can lift dreams from nothing to reality...
keeping them ever before the eyes....

Like one silent voices burst into song, the name
strikes the ear

And the sound of it rushes like a wild thing and
takes its place as the core of even the minutest
part of being.

Music has wings. It moves upon the wings of intuition
and thought.

Music is the Ambassador of the Airy Kingdom.

Sound... Cosmic Vibration.... Life

Pure life like pure blood is negative.
It is time to consider the negative planes of existence.
It is time to consider Music as a plane of wisdom

and a weapon of defense against the past and the
condemnations of the past.

Blood when negative is pure.
The negative is the symbol of the pure.
The Music of the past is positive Music in the same
way the past is symbolized by the positive. RA

BLACK SONG WEST

by Stanley Crouch

HORACE TAPSCOTT & THE COMMUNITY CULTURAL ORCHESTRA

Horace Tapscott, pianist, composer and leader of L.A.'s big Black Music band, the Community Cultural Orchestra, is one of the Black Artists who understands what the Black Renaissance is really about: A structural reordering of Black Communities along heavier standards, purer ways of living, changes of values, for, as LeRoi Jones has pointed out, in certain African languages the descriptive phrase for a man's death is, "He want west (white)." And what's happening is that Black today is about advancing across the country, as a Nation, as Black. Black everywhere. That is, culturally talking, the white man has convinced all people that New York is the cultural center of the country. We have allowed him to do this, to centralize the arts as he has government. Bu , as a trombonist in Tapscott's orchestra told me, "The place to be is where the Black Man is, and that's all over the world." Understood, but understanding without moving is suicide, and move is what we <u>must</u> do now: Must <u>make</u> every place, nationwide, <u>wherever</u> Black People are, <u>the</u> place to be. A nationwide cultural strain that will reap the recognition of Black People. The others are not important, just "Support of your own would do it," as Tapscott says. For it is a tragedy of expressive imprisonment that Black Artists accept the standards set up by he who has never had an authentic, openly truthful art form on the american continent, save a highly sophisticated system of thievery. That is, New York is only where <u>white men</u> say you should be to <u>prove</u> your ability and, as a young drummer told me, "Compete with them other cats for those jobs." Can you dig that? Prove yourself, not so you can better do what you were born towards, but so you can compete. That shouldn't even be in it, for Art is for everybody, not some way of establishing one's self as a "star"--that is, the Artist is talking about ways to <u>live</u>, and living, the way of breathing and touching, loving and moving Godward, has nothing to do with competition--and as we know, no one competes or creates a whole system of competing with God but the white man, one that has endured (or WE have endured) to this point anyway wherein the only tender thing thought of is the folding of a dollar in somebody's ass pocket. But there's a place we must build, we Black People and Artists. We must make a Nation and lock people out of the prisons, concrete or otherwise, which the white man has built. Horace Tapscott understands this (in fact, much of what was written above is his influence shooting through my mouth), understands it well, and has suffered because of it.

Recently, the white musicians' union, Local 47 (I say white musicians' union because the grays are the only ones they REALLY get jobs and work for--though there's no doubt Shelley Manne and others have long conversations to explain it), that organization, whiteballed Tapscott and made it law that anyone known playing with him would not be able to get work in any club in Los Angeles. This is a move to destroy what he has been trying to do: Free musicians to a point wherein they can get work on the basis of independent merit, not the number of asses kissed nor the funny styled fickleness of a racist structure. He must have scared them by not paying dues and talking against them, for, you see, independent darkies distress white people, and they will do almost anything they deem necessary to keep the fetters tight, Samson blinded and making bread for somebody else. But Tapscott will continue to grow, and, regardless of the obstacles, will only become stronger--and that thing, strength, should be the primary kinship amongst Black People. The musicians who work with Tapscott are examples of this. They, who sometimes call themselves the Underground Musicians and Artists Association, UGMA, are as determined as Horace is to make it free of the man.

Now let me give you some background on Tapscott (it has been a long time, hasn't it?). He is a brilliant pianist with a style coming from his way only--and make no mistake behind local corny radio stations like KBCA, he can PLAY. I heard him working with a trio one night at the Tropicana (gangster land, like the IT Club), and it was truly a cultural event: Another way of looking at the world through the piano, not just the chromatics and fourths and minor seconds that have become the foul replacement for copying Bud Powell. He took one solo on "The Song is You" that was so fantastic it might have even moved white people, had any been there. But, as with Los Angeles, it was nearly an empty club, though the music was bigger that this whole country town. Strange, trilling runs, broken rhythms that SWUNG as opposed to floated, reworking of chord changes for sharper statements and tenor heavy romanticism: The woman I was with commented, "He sounds like a tender man." It was that definite. And if you had heard the intro he played to Jitterbug Waltz, you'd be as wired up behind his playing as I am. He was accompanied by two other masters, bassist Dave Bryant and drummer Clarence Johnston who's got the hoo doo down. It was beautiful and even made the foul "freaked out" stuff the Tropicana calls "decoration" disappear. And Tap's been playing like this for a long time, though the average Black "jazz" fan on the street has never heard of him. But then a lot of the musicians don't dig him either because he PLAYS (and if you know anything about the jazz world, jealousy is a bitch got her clutches in a lot of hearts), plays, and doesn't go for just anything since bullshit's a bargain on the open market. That is, TOM. And, like I said way back there, now Horace has an Orchestra: The Community Cultural Orchestra, the heaviest large group in Los Angeles, the most often unemployed, and the most beautiful. All Black. ALL POWER. ALL LYRICISM. ALL SPIRIT. I'm finished, the rest of this will be Tapscott talking.

This band has all the Black Culture in it, and that's what it's for: For all of it. And reach out, stretch it all across the country. This is what it should be. We use the orchestra to have the people in the Black Community to see that they have something to contribute to whatever there is to contribute to the society. It's an educational thing primarily. Like everything, it's a hassle: They throw things, those things at you. To destroy you. The structure goes about its clever ways: Namely, the union. We could have our own things, be supported by our own, but that has a familiar sound, you dig, to <u>them</u>. Violence. We could dig a union if all of us were working. That's what we're in the process of doing, getting together. Like all them Black cats that can play so good fall to the wayside behind economic warfare. You shouldn't be looked at as a musician really anyway, more as a story teller, since that's what you are. We'd like the Orchestra to be seen as an institution, not just a band.

I want to talk a little bit about Black Arthur (Blythe). He's here now, he's alive, a lot of people have heard of him, but they don't come out to hear him. He's screaming a lot of things. Some of it's love, greed, some of it's lust, Saturday morning, a lot of things. He's got a masterful sound and a lot of things happening and he's not even known.

One of our drummers (the orchestra uses three), Everette Brown's at the Casbah and some people might know him because he's at a club, <u>one</u> of the clubs that'll hire musicians, while the other cats out there dying like dogs. You know, and if you do get in one, it's one of those things where you can't even play your instrument. I just don't think that all the cats that can play should be serenading tinkling glasses and back alley rendevous. If we had a place to play, there wouldn't be any need to classify, it'd just be people listening to <u>their</u> music. Musicians would be recognized while they're alive,

had a clipping of when Coltrane died, and do you know she actually asked me who John Coltrane was. A Black chick, a nigguh broad asked me that. The most sensible thing she said was, "Was he a friend of yours," I said, "Yeah." Most folks know Lester Robertson cause he's with Gerald Wilson, infact, he's his brother, by blood and looks. They have no idea he's one of the finest musicians in the country. And that ain't no kind of pride, no where. The way he plays trombone. Awareness is actually, now, our job, to help them realize, not just the laymen, the musicians too, all the Black People, me too. Most of the hipsters think Dave Bryant is a vocalist. This should be titled "An open letter to the Los Angeles Blacks, then the country."

I asked him about the problems of selling out.

In music, they say, "If you would write this with a Motown beat to it. It's beautiful, it's a beautiful arrangement, but most of all, it doesn't have any electric guitars in it. And if it's more than three minutes long, it's grotesque. We can't play that on the air." Most of all, we need communications in the Black Community so more kinds of music can be heard by the Black People. They're there, they're intelligent. Then when you're seen on the street you wouldn't have to be subjected to "Hey man," which is just a step up from "Hey boy." And on the gig, you get asked to play "Bill Bailey Would You Please Come Home," or "Do you know 'The Shadow of Your Smile'?"

(I commented that that was Gil Fuller's tune, that the underground was aware of it and so was Tapscott probably, but he said nothing. What was there to say.)

Or then there's, "You can work at this resort, but do two of the people in the group sing?" So you're taken from being the musician to being the court jester, that is if you're interested in playing in King Arthur's Court. We'd like to imagine ourselves playing in a place like South Park. Some place right in the middle of the Black Community.

The music, the newer type things--Ornette, Dolphy, cats like that--has been out here a long time, from back when Bird was here, but it's been in garages and places like that where the people couldn't hear it. Some more pressures they can lay on you is when they freeze you out from gigs when you want to gig. This is pressures that come from your own colleagues, so-called. A lot of these pressures come from the structure telling cats, "Stray, instead of play." Or, "Sell out." Economically, the musician goes under the heading of "hidden poverty," overlooked, a nice black suit on the weekend, having a ball, no responsibilities. The invidible man within the invisible man. Shouldn't be: We shouldn't even be within anything invisible. Dimensional invisibility, on and on, anything else, I asked.

Why don't you listen. That's all.

* *

So there you have it. LISTEN. Later on, in other columns, I'll talk at length about some of the people in the Orchestra. Black Arthur and Lattus McNeeley, two of the best alto players anywhere. James Lee, like Bobby Bradford and Walter Lowe, one of the trumpet players who would turn the thing around but is hidden behind the blank newspapers of the mass media. Kenny Humphries, a trombonist so far away from Jay Jay, Grachan, Roswell Rudd and the others I could only call him an innovator, though I doubt anything of the sort's even on his mind, just music probably. Then there's Lester Robertson, whom I'll interview singly. Everett Brown's a better drummer than almost anybody you can think of. So is Leroy Brooks. Pianist Gwint Coleman has a two-handed way of stretching out that would buck the eyes of most bomp bomp in the left hand piano players. He'll be interviewed singly also. Goddam! there are so many people out here. So many. And so beautiful. Anybody interested in booking the band into their place should call Tapscott at 294-7835.

* *

Next column, if I can catch up with him, I'll interview Walter Lowe, who is, along with Bobby Bradford, James Lee and Don Cherry, one of THE trumpet players in the music. ANYWHERE.

INQUIRY

DO YOU THINK THE MAFIA KILLED OTIS REDDING ??????????????????????????????

DO YOU THINK THE MAFIA KILLED OTIS REDDING ??????????????????????????????

DO YOU THINK THE MAFIA KILLED OTIS REDDING ??????????????????????????????

DO YOU THINK THE MAFIA KILLED OTIS REDDING ??????????????????????????????

DO YOU THINK THE MAFIA KILLED OTIS REDDING ??????????????????????????????

DO YOU THINK THE MAFIA KILLED OTIS REDDING ??????????????????????????????

DO YOU THINK THE MAFIA KILLED OTIS REDDING ??????????????????????????????

DO YOU THINK THE MAFIA KILLED OTIS REDDING ??????????????????????????????

DO YOU THINK THE MAFIA KILLED OTIS REDDING ??????????????????????????????

DO YOU THINK THE MAFIA KILLED OTIS REDDING ??????????????????????????????

DO YOU THINK THE MAFIA KILLED OTIS REDDING ??????????????????????????????

DO YOU THINK THE MAFIA KILLED OTIS REDDING ??????????????????????????????

DO YOU THINK THE MAFIA KILLED OTIS REDDING ??????????????????????????????

DO YOU THINK THE MAFIA KILLED OTIS REDDING ??????????????????????????????

DO YOU THINK THE MAFIA KILLED OTIS REDDING ??????????????????????????????

DO YOU THINK THE MAFIA KILLED OTIS REDDING ??????????????????????????????

WRITE THE CRICKETS

Box 663

Newark, N. J.

THE SILENT PROPHET

Trane

must have

died

a thousand

times

trying to tell

us

what it was

all about

but we were

so busy

dancing

we couldn't hear

his music.

NORMAN JORDAN

HARLEM COLUMN # 1

Willis Jackson's at the Baron.
His group's an old, big, organ-
-guitar-drum-saxophone sound.
Heavy-beat music that still
makes me think of tap-dancers.
The jew-owned Baron undergoes
renovations to hold more black people.
Where I'm sitting I can't see the drummer,
his sound's like a machine.
Willis sound like Lester's sound- relaxed.
Willis plays "jitter-bug" sounds,
from the time when jazz'(best)
musicians used to play what black people
danced to.
The way the people moved inspired their
sounds.
Today its the way the musicians think,
and feel and see.
Now sounds different from then, too,
cause the white man split black music
into ½ dozen categories for ease of
handling/analysis/capitalization/exploitation.
It used to be all one thing.
Willis heart ain't in it -
maybe its because its only the day after
off-night,
or maybe its cause the place is ½ empty,
so they're not cooking
as impressively as they will on Friday.
I finished drinking my admission price and
I'll probably go back.

GOSSIP

Why only organ trios in black communities? .... Where is the new music and the new musicians?........... Where should black musicians play?............. What is a night club?............ Why should our musicians play in them?....... Why isn't Pharoah receiving any dough off Tauhid?????????.......... Why don't black musicians turn down contracts with beast recording, and record with brothers? .... Jihad Productions, soon to be releasing two volume albums, volume 1 Rap Brown & Sun Ra, volume 2 LeRoi Jones & Pharoah Sanders, Albert Ayler called Black Renaissance also, Black Mass, play by LeRoi Jones w/Spirit House Movers and the Music of Sun Ra & his Myth Science Arkestra......... many, many more sides to come. Salaam till next time.

The Cricket

DRAMA

SPIRIT HOUSE MOVERS

The Black Repertory Theater
The Living Word!

We bring BLACK ART, anywhere, and more,
yelling "We Bad"!!!!!

FOR FURTHER INFORMATION WRITE:

SPIRIT HOUSE
33 STIRLING STREET
NEW ARK, N. J.

Recent Productions: Black Mass, Home on the Range, Great Goodness of Life;

skits, Insurrection, War Hero, Junkie, and more by LeRoi Jones

##

Words, are words, meant to TEACH!!!!!!!!!!

TO say RAISE!!!! RAISE!!!! RAISE!!!!

Tho they are must be righteous projections,

good (images) to make future, be a Black Nation.

JOURNAL
OF
BLACK
POETRY

For all Black People everywhere!
Write: Journal of Black Poetry
1308 Masonic Ave. #4
San Francisco, Calif.

TRUTH
TRUTH TRUTH
TRUTH TRUTH
TRUTH TRUTH
TRUTH TRUTH

Issue 4
(1969)

111–182

CRICKET

TRIPPIN'

A NEED FOR CHANGE

THE CRICKET

BLACK MUSIC in EVOLUTION !!!!

Mtengenezaji mchango: Imamu Baraka, Larry Neal, A.B. Spellman

Maelekeano: Sun Ra, Milford Graves, Cecil Taylor

Santuri waarifu: Gaston Neal, Wash., D.C.; James Stewart, Philadelphia; Clyde Halisi, LA; Don L. Lee, Chicago; Norman Jordan, Cleveland; Roger Riggins, Philadelphia; Mtume, LA; Ronnie Gross, Paterson; Ben Caldwell, New York; Mwanafunzi Katibu, New Ark, more to come

Subscribe to:

THE CRICKET

Box 663

New Ark, New Jersey

contents

COVER BY: BEN CALDWELL

PHOTOS BY: BILLY ABERNATHY

DAN DAWSON

The Black musician must, as any other revolutionary artist, be a projector whose message reflects the values of the culture from which his creation owes its existence. He must be the antennae which receives the visions of a better life and time and transmits those visions into concrete realities through the use of sound and substance (each time must be a lecture via entertainment). The Black musician must be both Spiritual, in that he must strive to create visions faster than the present and perpetuate the higher values of man, and Secular in that <u>his music must not go so far out that it transcends the ability of the people to grasp its meaning and message</u>. Therefore the music evolved from the artist would possess simultaneously an aesthetic appreciation as well as a political interpretation of where we are and where we shall be.

Although the artists were traditionally the first revolutionaries (rejected European form and emphasized African feeling) never-the-less we have allowed white people to label and be critics of our direction and development. While we refine our movement they define our movement. How long will we stand by and permit, by statement or silence, non-creative beings to comment as authorities on the worth or unworth of our conceptualizations of how music is to be played (like a Liberace discussing why McCoy Tyna ain't a righteous piano player because he doesn't play 200 year old stuff like Swan Lake or some other static sickness of that un-nature). The same determination and imagination utilized to make black music what it is and will be must also be channelled and perceived in other aspects of the art form. First we must have a change in definition. As the creators it is up to us to define our creation. If we continuously allow white people to define our space as artists we don't deserve to occupy that space as the artist. When will we begin to employ our own resourcefulness by bringing into existence our own terminology to compliment our music. For example, the word Jazz is a white mis-interpretation of what we were doing. By definition Jazz or Jazzy means sex or sexy (check it out in an old Webster) because that's what his concept of music and movement lead him to believe. According to him, any music that led to movement of the body, the highest expression being that of dancing, was automatically looked upon as a physical description of sex rather than a spiritual display of symbiosis. Dancing, to Black people, is the ritualized act of becoming one with that which they are involved with. "We of US organization under the guidance and leadership of Maulana Karenga, have as an act of self-determination chosen to define our music as "Trippin'", as oppossed to using the word Jazz, for that is exactly what the artist does when he plays and involves us in his journey in search of new sounds, new colors, and new realities beyond the comprehensions of this dimension." It is difficult to believe that even at this late date after the appearance of the vanguard artist who laid the foundation on which the music of today derives its main frame of reference, we still allowed white people to term that movement, avante-garde (as if some European had started something). I hardly perceived any French in Coltrane from "My Favorite Things" to "Cosmic Music", in Sun Ra's conception of "When Angels Speak of Love", in Ornette, Cecil Taylor, Pharoah or any of the expandera referred to as avante-garde (we had best <u>guard</u> against using slave labels).

If we are to be truly innovators of a New Music we must at the same time be revolutionary by elevating the aspirations of our people through the inspirations of our music. This can only be accomplished by the artists committment to the ideals of his people and his dedication to creativity and change. We must view our music and the world through a Black perspective, an endless energy force, which will lead us to the establishment of a criteria from which to judge the merits and shortcomings of our music. Only in accordance with a Black value system will the artist be supplied with a means for a correct interpretation of the reality and relevance of the music the music makers make.

MTUME

INTEGRATION MUSIC

Re: Jimi Hendrix

Sly & F.S.

5th Dim

The principle is the same as Guess Who Went Out To Lunch. It is for the money#! But for the feeling (as money. Money as feeling, or, more clearly, Money, as a way of life. Fahamu?) Money, here, and "success" are interchangeable. Success in a particular vein. JH, of course, being an actual freak. The rest as artfull dodgers, from real, all the way back into white shadows.

Interesting, in that it proposes the deadly "millenium". It is said that Bobby Seals digs Bobby Dylan. We think they should make an album together. It's a "natural"!

Imamu Ameer Baraka

MONK at COUNT BASIE'S

Monk is fluid time--the fin-

    gering melo-dee

the crafted funk speaks

behind and under looney tune changes.

he came round midnight

        the sperm splattered notes

tripping into Basie's dark womb.

and there were wonders here: time spiraling

in the beat, fluidly, the September Monk

lurks chanting behind the horn.

chants mean and nasty: "yo mammy too...and who you blew"

                and dee Blah da to you too

tell it: dee blah da for the mysterioso weird ones.

the holy monks who died of O. D.

in the scared arteries of the city.

dee blah da for the ones with heavy collars

dying of clap from banging white girls.

dee blah da for the blue soul Trane

who sped us East, turning us in on ourselves.

dee blah da for the crafted funk

and honky-tonk bud the hip cat's stud.

this is Monk's tune, the black angel of the changes!
heard the lyric pulse, backed and reshifted it,
rechewed the broken lyric into a singular language
system/ dee blah da/ dee dee blaah/ dee blah da
for the dead dope sniffers
and the white paper critics hustling
their shit in the pages of Downbeat
and Jazz magazines.
Monk shits on them...a dynamite chord
explodes blasting leonard feather's head off...
DE BLAH DA!!!

BLUE MONK

the last set was a soft set
mist covering the windows
amorphous shadows on seventh avenue
an opaque song flickering against
the backdrop of blue ritual color
way way down low now
way way down now a silent meanness
    we
      are
    bent in
      prayer.

Larry Neal

karma/PHAROAH SANDERS

The temple had a round spiraling dome and I stood with my father's spirit listening to Pharoah cascade through alcoves and spectrums of light; and yes the light came in many colors, the black shatterings full released, some under spirits churning too. My father had never heard Pharoah in his time so he wept upon hearing him, and raised his hands in prayer; he then said some words I couldn't understand. but the dome was spiraling gold figures filterings and flickerings in the shattering black love. It was a good place to be, in the temple again and yes the light breaking against mosaic, wind song and Dahomey memories; father, the sun, the energy principle.

Pharoah, the purest spirit sings to us on this album. Takes us to beautiful places. Your brothers and sisters are there; it is sunday church picnic time in Mali or Dakar; or alabama talk, revival time perhaps. Saw you in Timbuctoo, remember? Or Chicago on 72nd street. It was all about spirals of energy my father said over my ear in the temple while listening to Pharoah's cosmic chorus of daddy and mommy tribe. Pharoah, the purest spirit is our vision. When these bodies pass, one great desire we should have is to become a phrase in one of Pharoah's songs, to dance all inside of them feeling total and holy. We are Timbuctoo memory. Camel walking prophets and soothsayers. Malik, the warrior god. We are one long song of love. Teach Pharoah. Teach us Pharoah. Teach how to live.

Pharoah has become one long beautiful song. What we get here is a tribal chorus; the sum total of a people's song. There is memory here and future realities. Some of your cousins and the folks on your mother's side lurk here too, doing the belly rub in dark corners. Holy sinners march through this song singing Allah; and the Great Serpent churns there too. Hey, remember lemonade Sundays and the first smell of love-body? Remember the star night, some explosion shattering love come. Perhaps in a time before this time. Lady wonder magic toy; and the drums Oba gave you, Timbuctoo memory, and Dahomey smiles. Sweet Aisha and Helen and fiery Evelyn and Great Mamma floating skyward and sea-chains and the dead devil language and Nat and Sojourner and cotton and moonshine and Buddy and Jelly Roll and Bessie and Lester and Billie and Bird and Brownie and Johnnie and Trane and Paul and all of the yous doing ju-ju dance and cakewalk and lolligagging under a God crowded sky. Pharoah speaks to the whole experience, we need to protect him. He needs a temple to pray in, that's what my father's spirit said to me. He needs the children of Lenox Avenue to dance-fly on his songs. He needs to be played in the ears of cop-out negroes. He would rescue Eldridge and Bobby. He would tear away our weaknesses. He would give us the sun strength; let the real panther bellow out, speak the wisdom of the black stone, some cycles we travel passing from mother to mother and father to father. He would make us dig ourselves. He would verify our instincts, telling us really what we have always knew but were too afraid to sing.

Outer space. Beyond your self. Stardust from tomorrow. But everybody knows better. Ski-glasses. The brothers and sisters in the band wear ski-glasses. It's a cold mother, now. Snowy cold and white. Out there, beyond the stage: white, incomprehension, blankness, jiggling when the music says jag.

But they get into it. And it's outer space. Thrust. Rocking back and forth. Rocking. Straining. The stress. Til it almost hurts the ears, but it's together. Moves you. The out/ fits. Fit for space. Fit for tomorrow. Space-cloaks shimmering, shiney, bright colored. Tomorrow's stardust, just you wait and see. Sun Ra, forcing it, pushing it on. Hats geared down over the eyes, set for space. Outer space. Sun Ra, fingers and fists flying, works that organ...

Total control. Seasoned space travelers, that's the feeling you get, as you listen, as you watch the brothers move about the stage, changing instruments, blowing, beating, shaking. And the two sisters: dancing, singing, keep you geared, take you where the band is headed. Asking you, "If we can come from nowhere here, why not go from somewhere...there." Expansion.

Clouds passing above. A few stars. Spotlights across the sky. The sound: Shooting stars, whirling galaxies of sound. Expansion.

"...fresh
galaxies spinning in the
dead brain of the world,"

--Mkalimoto

Over-toned by Sun Ra on that organ; or a brother sweeping you bellows from what looks like a home made horn; or the sisters, singing, singing un-earthly.

Changes:

Basic Afro-american rhythms; hip-swinging tunes; humor (all kinds), a good groove, that makes you know maybe everything is allright despite the velocity, the newlyness, the range of the voyage.

Songs: "Spaceways, travelling...the spaceways..." Hymns, of a kind. Our kind. It's the Nile again. It's green again. The Disk of Day over Egypt. A time for standing, a time for dancing -- and thrust, of growth...until all ways are open.

Instruments. Things that click, shimmer, cling, blast, bellow, wail, humm... it's all there, the sounds we know, knew, and will come to know. And together, so easily together that you think it <u>must</u> be that way. Until you realize that nobody else has got it that way, are not able to get it or even near it. Until you realize that it is a "higher discipline" that brings this together. It's "ensemble": Paintings, weavings, color, poetry, song, dancing: VISIONING. It's heroic Long-March music like we haven't heard since when. It's us in outer space, sitting down, tired, with Universe charts, not clear where we are but sure of getting there. It's pyramid-building, world-construction, Universe-revision. But all these names are small, because it gets beyond barb-wire frontiers, ghettoes, bloated categories, things like that. It's outer space. Comes outside the stage. Into you. These gemini players. Players. Space - players. Spacers. Space-makers. For us:

What we never had for so long, space, outer space. Or much space at all. squeezed so tight. from the slaveship to the shack to the tenement. No space to really move. No space to really function. Sun Ra & Co. herald Space To Come, Freedom, to move, to live again as ourselves. Expansion.

And future talk is ordering talk. Getting pretty much what we order and ordering pretty much what we get, future has to be incorporated into today as surely as history. When we hear a brother say, "A nigger ain't never <u>been</u> shit, a nigger ain't never <u>going</u> to be shit," we know he has no knowledge of his past, and no past = no future. Sun Ra is future/ ALTER/ what's coming. Tomorrow's breath, breathing. Getting ready.

****

But it was a visitation to have Sun Ra here. This Herald in San Fran, otherwise known as The End Of The World. Where the white people come for their last hopes, then jump, one way or another, off that bridge. San Fran, where the West ends. After here there is nothing but East, nothing but home, down home and Home.

That's where you go with Sun Ra and his bad bad Co., down home, through the Caribbean, Brazil, other planets, other planes, to Home, its beauty, and beyond.

JOE GONCALVES

SCENES/BASIC MAKEUP OF THE MUSIC

I

if we could dig
the impetus
of a revolution/ ary
art
life would be
the congenial
clarification
of all things
as of now (independent of past de-
          finitions)

the western aesthetic
falls
& angels
take forms
that represent
the beauty of
our
creation

its time (jackie mclean--long & clean)
right now
to build
to assemble
for a black

vision

of substance

II

we must

carry

the weight of

trane & eric

whip the skies

with the glory

of cosmic spiritual

vi/ bra/ tions

III

bop is dead

it can

be viewed historically

perhaps

sonny simmons

has

to get

relationships

together

so the music

can get

even

stronger

work to be done here

work   to be   done   here

IV

the new black music
sees
the future
it is the future
of what
we will be

musicians
gotta start
keep'en up
with what
their
music
implies

come on brothers!!

---Roger Riggins---

A Consideration of The Art of Ornette Coleman

To those of you who are not at all familiar with Ornette Coleman's musical methodology, may I add this bit of information. He has, among other things included in his musical methodology the personal handling of many instruments, which to all existing evidence he never acquired any formal training on. Notably the trumpet and the violin. He has, I've been told, even used the musette in a concert given the early part of last year. This suggests to me that the purely autodidactic nature of his genuius must be taken into account in understanding his art.

When the album, THE EMPTY FOXHOLE[1] appeared it aroused considerable controversy. The controversy emanated from what was considered the ill-advisability of Ornette Coleman and the producers of the album of releasing such an album. The album displayed the work of Ornette's son, Ornette Denardo, who was then ten years old.

All of the "inside" "mainstream" musicians denounced it as a rank insult to professional stature of the jazz musician, this utilization of an obvious inept who they protested (and rightly so, within the context of their particular musical orientation) possessed neither the depth or technique essential to professional musical maturation.

I have presumed to write this in Ornette's behalf, knowing fully that Ornette needs no such justification professionally, aesthetically or otherwise. I herewith ask Brother Ornette to forgive my presumptiousness.

Yet, in my defense this paper is as much a statement of my own aesthetic objectives, as it is a consideration of what I presume is Ornette's.

Personality, to some may seem out of place in a piece on revolutionary art or art in a revolutionary context. The argument being that revolutionary imperatives preclude personality. But nothing of this sort occurs. Often, this misunderstanding stems from the person's belief that individualism (which is rejected in the revolutionary context) and personality are synonymous. Maulana Karenga[2] said that individuality is "me" in spite of everybody else, and personality is "me" with everybody, in relationship to others. In terms of his craft, in terms of how the Ornette Coleman "me" relates to revolution, the thrust of his personality must be considered in its most obvious condition e.g. in the manner he uses his material and what it indicates in the total role in revolution. For aside from all of the categories the establishment insist on wanting to place the new Black music into, the only verbal approximation of its aesthetic portents is its conceptual redact of the Black world black revolution envisions. Whether he sees his productions in this light or not, need not matter. I rather doubt that he does. But let us proceed now and invent a rationale for his method. Let us say that this artist has caught some glint of the conception he is attempting to actualize. He has worked it out and through a particular instrument. Then he relinquishes that instrument and taking up a totally different and unfamiliar instrument proceeds to apply the working out of his conception on the new instrument, attacking his ignorance of that instrument's mechanism alone, without any previous knowledge of the procedure of its mechanics or of its methodology. Imposing, in fact, his own methodology on the instrument. This is the sui generis Black artist in the new Black revolutionary music. He has, and he must, literally exile himself from the formal (an euphemism for white or European) musical structures. He must abandon all previous European musical methodologies and seek for himself the OM of creative beauty that reposes in our Black culture. This is the meaning of "freedom". An in terms of not only ridding himself of an alien and restrictive system he must be an artist, a revolutionary artist in the broad sense of the word, in this case a musician in a true sense of the word. Thinking across and controlling all aspects of the category of music. He must avoid the stylization that the "mainstream jazz-art" nurtured, with the kind of "individualist" packaging the economic profit machinery grounded in the gear-teeth of the American mallophaga. Thus Ornette avoided the inevitable stereotypal and repetitiveness working through a single instrument develops. By these terms the scope of Black revolutionary creation must entail, not only the historical and -ultural rejection of the European tempered musical tradition but its methodology as well.

The truly Black revolutionary creative thinkers must treat their art in terms of the larger malleability of its material; across the entire range of their particular category. In the context of the new Black music, in terms of what one might call the new Black aesthetic critique, the new Black artist must posit the primary aesthetic principles of his art on the appropriately termed notion of "freedom" from a white western musical hegemony.

Creation, is then what conception aspires matter to be. Matter, in this case is what music is when it is heard. Working through one instrument restricts the extent of the realization and development of the conception. The instrument, in a sense "freezes" the elements of the conception. Whereas, a totally different and strange instrument would only resist the working out of the conception because of the musicians ignorance of that particular instrument's mechanism. This, he purposely welcomes. It challenges the imprintation he hopes to realize. This is improvisation in the new Black innovative and revolutionary meaning; creating a magnificant new Black music for new Black people.

Jimmy Stewart

FOOTNOTES:

1- The Empty Foxhole, BlueNote Records BLP 4246/84246

2- Ron Karenga and Black Cultural Nationalism by Maulana Ron Karenga; Negro Digest, January, 1968

The Outer Bridge

In the half-between world

Dwell they, the sound-scientist

Mathematically precise. . . . . . .

They speak of many things

The tone scientists

Architects of planes of discipline.

Sun Ra

EULOGY FOR TOMMY

Tommy was a very spiritual human being. His poems show this. He was a poet, a lover of man, a seeker of truth. He sought for God and the Spiritual Life: he was moving towards the East, towards Eastern religion - - the religion of Africa, the unity with the souls of our ancestors; he was seeking to communicate with God.

Around his neck he wore the Ankh, the African Cross, the symbol of Life and Resurrection. Tommy had his own way of seeing and communicating with God and the Spiritual Universe - - and he was seeking to return to his roots.

Often we talked, in New York, and later in San Francisco, about Eastern religions and Black music and art. He loved our music and musicians such as John Coltrane whom he saw as a highly spiritual, Eastern brother. Tommy was, again, heading in this direction. He very much admired the religion of West Africa, the Yoruba faith.

Slender, wiry, yet muscular, he would sit up smoking late into the New York night discussing these things with Roy, his brother, and other friends. His quiet eyes would and could always grasp or see into the heart of another person....He was quiet, but when he spoke, he was really <u>saying something</u>...He was a Soul Brother!

He lived his life wild and free with the rhythm that made Coltrane blow his Great Horn into the face of God, or James Brown scream about trouble in this life, or lost love, or Otis Redding calling for Respect, Respect for the Black man, who was getting himself together, coming into his own, like Tommy tried to do; standing up for his soul-felt dignity, standing tall or walking into the misty night: Tommy speaking to all of us with his quiet eyes seeing it all, trying to put it together, this life, trying to make it beautiful to live.

When Tommy came to San Francisco for a visit during the Christmas - New Years holidays, he was very depressed, very beat down; he was trying to stand tall, be a man, and this thing was whipping him, whipping him bad. I could see it in his eyes which had grown sad and tired...He spoke with difficulty where once he was clear and outspoken. He spoke of how sick some of our people were, how tired he had become from trying to wake them up. We walked and talked about it; I wanted him to unburden his troubles on me so that I could help to lift his spirits as much as possible. I could see then that it was beginning to kill him - - inside. The Deathwish was there: it always comes with extreme suffering. The loneliness, the pain...unable to really communicate with anyone, except his brother, Roy, and one or two others, he was turning in upon himself.

As I go back over these events in my mind, I wonder how many of us <u>really</u> knew or understood Tommy -- or saw him for what he was: a Poet, a man of Soul, who spoke about the inner being of man, his feelings, emotions, spiritual desires. (America has long been known for murdering its artists, musicians, and poets -- its finest, most sensitive souls.)

He was groping and growing, trying to see beyond the phoniness and fronts into a new way, a more human, natural rhythm. He wanted books and writings about the East and Africa; he valued these more than material things. I gave him what I had. I had noticed how he had a hunger for books: to read, to learn, to understand.

Tommy, a young warrior in the America of the 'sixties, a Black man searching for the Truth in life, seeking wisdom.

He is gone now, gone from us all -- except in that deep, special part of ourselves we call our heart; he is gone from sight. Tommy, my own special hero: poet and Soul-warrior wearing the sacred Ankh of his ancestors, digging it all, telling the truth, being righteous deep inside. After today, we will return to our lives taking a small part of him with us -- our memories. Do not forget him, but do not mourn too long, for he would want us to keep on growing and struggling to live, and find our place in the sun -- as Stevie Wonder sings. He can rest now from his hard labor, for he is one with his brother, Larry, Malcolm, Coltrane, and Otis Redding -- at last linking up with God and the Ancestors. His life was short in terms of years, but he traveled far along the Path of Life, growing, and groping towards his own special understanding, our Tommy . . . and now in God may he find the Peace and Beauty that he searched for and discovered in his gentle poems.

Askia Muhammed Toure

"SAY BE AND BEHOLD IT IS"

The agony of it all is a blessing
The blessing of it all is blackness
The blackness of it all is a spirit
The spirit of it all is cosmic
The cosmic of it all is energy
The energy of it all is Allah
Allah is Allah, Allah is all
Allah is

Haasan Oqwiendha Fum al Hut

POSITIVE BLACK MUSIC

As the Black Musician awakens his intuition, he finds before him a vast world of musical expressions. The further he moves away from the corny toot-toot-toot of the western world, the more real and beautiful his music becomes.

It's true the black musician has been able to hold on to more of his originality than most black artists; yet, when we hear and experience some of the unfolding black talents of today we have to acknowledge that we've been derailed further than some of us would like to admit.

Black music, as well as all constructive art, <u>must be free</u>, and at the same time, it <u>must contain order</u> a positive harmony on the physical, mental and spiritual level.

Too many Brothers (with good intentions) have gone off into an abstract, eccentric, psychedelic, tantrum, doing anything to be different, killing themselves from the inside out. What these Brothers fail to realize is that we are complete, positive BEINGS with a definite purpose and that the freedom which we are searching for is universal harmony - a way of expressing ourselves that is as natural and necessary as breathing or making love.

As Pharoah Sanders and the Brothers who created Tauhid point out very clearly, meaningful black art can and must be free; by the same stick it must have a goal, a purpose. Listening to these Brothers, we know every sound is a planned move, a precise expression, but the execution of each note and the total effect, is a perfectly free and beautiful statement.

Besides objective harmony and mutual respect, these Brothers are blessed with the "we" conscious - The Zodiac frame of mind - which gives each brother a chance to do his thing without exploiting or stepping on his Brother's toe, a one-in-all, all-in one relationship. For anyone who has heard the album, the result of this conscious-freedom speaks for itself.

In our art, along with our day to day experiences, we must keep in mind that we live in a very complete (all praises to Allah) and orderly world, where Chance is a universal law unrecognized. Freedom is knowing and being in tune with the universe and its laws.

Norman Jordan

Listening to this album. Makes me tired. Its jive. Shepp hasn't, lost his, soul. Yet. But Devil Dogs can make this happen, think abt it Archie Shepp. You shd know. The elements, you draw near are the ones you become, try to be like. If you around people who smoke, and drink all the time then thats. All you will want, to please, do. Roswell Rudd, is confused, and hysterical each time he speaks. ("Plays") is what his whole essence is about. Along with Lust, Violence, and Money. The worship of these things. Archie Shepp thinks, it's hip to take an album cover photo w/death air flowin out his mouth. No values. And as Imamu teaches "Be conscious of the whole, and you will have the strength of the whole. The traditional disciplines, The ancient strengthens the mind, the body, the soul". Archie Shepp is away from these thoughts, miles. He need to come back to us. Before it's too late, let Rudds sensibility crawl in a corner and die. Donald Garrett/ Lewis Worrell contributed the only binder (Black Music Sense). Beever has been weakened by (he knows). If you see this side, pass it by for some Music. Black Music.

Mwanafunzi Katibu

TO MR. JONES - I HAD A VISION

Brothers and Sisters,

Listen. A few weeks ago I beared witness to my last Miracle; Here it is: Fear God and give glory to him for the hour of his judgement is come. Worship him that made the heaven and earth and the sea and the fountains of waters. Babylon is fallen, that great city because he made all nations drink of the wine of the wrath of her fornication. If any men worship the beast and his image and receive his mark in his forehead or in his hand the same shall drink of the wine of his fornication and the same shall drink of the wine of the wrath of God which is poured out without mixture into the cup of his indignation. Revelation 14:7:10

Let every soul be subjected unto the higher power for there is no power but of God. Roman 13:1

They have healed also the hurt of the daughrer people slightly, say peace, peace, peace when there is no peace. Jeremiah 6:14

I HAD A VISION

It was at night when I had this vision. In this vision there was a large object flying around with bright colors in a disc form. Immediately I thought of the flying scorpion that I had read about in the chapter of Revelation from the Holy Bible, but when the object started turning I saw that first it was flat then it turned sideways and started to shoot radiant colors at first then it would turn back to the same position. I was running with my brother when it aimed at us but it didn't touch us at all. I guess this is what they are calling the flying saucers. Anyway it was revealed to me that we had the right seal of God almighty in our forehead.

One morning I was awakened by all the kids upstairs running to the window because of a sound outside that was so piercing it was paralizing. It was revealed to me a few weeks later that it was Gabriel sounding the warning. This was the angel of Jesus standing on his right side, and that Gabriel is the spirit of sound and strength. The sound lasted for five minutes. Every thing will happen fast so be ready.

I dreamed of a man starting to make war with a lamb, the man suddenly looked around and there was a man standing with large swords on a disc throwing with perfection. It seemed to me like the magic of the creator. The swords had a bright color to then clear as a crystal. I remembered again the book of Revelations about how Jesus would come with a very sharp sword.

In a night vision I saw a very dark sky and I looked up and saw a large star falling as fast as it could move. Brothers and Sisters you see there is only Heaven and Earth. There is no other planets. The planet that they call Venus is Zion Hill, the home of God Almighty. That's why it is written he created the Heaven and Earth, the Sea and the Fountains of Waters and all the things therein. On the seventh day he rested. The seventh day he rested on is the Sabbath day, of which is the fourth commandment. Now we must follow the tenth commandment. This is the spiritual law of God Almighty. Now you see all the talk about other planets has only been an illusion. I say unto you that whosoever breaketh the tenth commandment is servants of sin. Brothers, watch the sex acts because your blood is your strength.

Elijah Mohammed is the true Prophet.

Cleanliness is Godliness. Don't forget that arguing with each other is bad because if you do the devil angel is laughing in the closet, so be careful. You see if you argue the Holy angels leave you because they are of oneness of harmony, so don't bring on the devil. The devil angel thrives off of uncleanliness, curse words, blasphemy, and discord.

In the forehead of Satan written across his forehead the word blasphemy is there. This is his name also so be very careful and respect God's laws, so you won't receive the devil's mark in your forehead or your right hand. I have seen a few people with the mark already so be very careful and God's angels will be with you even unto the end. Eat only the green things and no meat at all if possible. And pray always from your heart and God Almighty will hear you. If you do you won't be afraid of the terror by night nor for the arrow that flieth by day because he will always be at your side. Remember that contention and discord quench the spirit of prayer. Many grieve the spirit and drive Christ from their homes by giving way to impatience and passions. Thus saith the Lord ... If thou turn away they foot from the Sabbath, from doing thy pleasure on My behalf on My Holy day and call the Sabbath a delight the holy of the Lord, honorable; and shalt honor Him, not doing thine own pleasure, nor speaking thine own words; then shalt thou delight thyself in the Lord; and I shall cause thee to ride upon the high places of the earth, and feed thee with the heritage of Jacob thy father; for the mouth of the Lord hath spoken it." Read my friend.

I saw in a vision the new Earth built by God coming out of Heaven. Years ago they called it New Jerusalem. It was a solid foundation built by God himself. It is not like the foundation that we have now where men seek to kill each others spirit.

The vision I had of Jesus coming again, it was at night again; large clouds forming in the east and something said to me this is the way Jesus is coming. The Son of God would be coming in his father's name, God Almighty. So be ready when that time comes, because it could happen in the wink of an eye. Remember he said you know not the minute nor the hour, so let's be obedient children to God's Laws. We live in darkness now; God Almighty is the God of lights. You see there are mighty angels from Heaven and they are very large. Bright as the sun. Another way to describe it is like the color of lightening magnified ten times. So you'd better get ready for the bright lights that will appear in the sky. It has been written on the wall of the universe by God Almighty for me to see and give you this message. So don't transgress any of God's Laws. The time is at hand. Make up leaflets and pass out to all people Revelation 14, verse 7 to 10. This is very important that everybody should know this will save your soul and you will see a beautiful eternity. I'll have more to say next time. We must move this by chain letters and get it in the papers in as many parts of the U.S.A. as possible. This is very important. The time is now.

Albert Ayler

POEM FOR THE JOURNAL OF BLACK POETRY

The

Sun blows

change

shapes change

with slim silver

musician fingers

or slow dry raps

from desert poets

Black spirit

three

Aries, Leo

all must become

<u>one</u>

pass and future must become

<u>"eternal now"</u>

Change

a universal silouette

with star-crescent eyes

a Holy being

shaping the world

with cosmic love

& infinite black hands

The

Sun blows

change

shapes change

with slim silver

musician fingers

or slow dry raps

pt

Norman Jordan

respect

I've just been told that Brother Coleman Hawkins has died. What can I say. He was a man--he was a Black man who blew a tenor saxaphone in the most outstanding manner. He was one of the fathers of invention on his instrument.

But why speak in a mellow tone. I've seen this man play to an audience of ten on a shallow bandstand at the Five Spot Cafe in New York City (and none of those in the audience were spooks!). This never should have been--it must never happen to one of our artists again!

I think it would be rather dubious to discuss the life history and accomplishments. The man was a giant.

rains of beauty
hit the soul
of those who
understand
the power of
truth &
talent

blackness
has a way
of showing
truth
hawk was a black
he was truth

---Roger Riggins---

Whistle For Pennies

Haartebeespoort* Dam! And song and dance would pierce the air celebrating the birth of a new year, the lyrics, with poetic precision, caressing, describing, exploring this experience with the robustness of released township passions. Happy New Year . . . Happy New Year! Kwa se kusuk'amaphepha . . . and the papers flew . . . isitimela siy'eOrlando . . . the train going to Orlando. Yes. Mbaqanga dubbed kwela by white critics who hear the music as nothing more than an expression of the noisy happiness of simple-minded township natives and a gold mine for recording companies. Fuduwa ousi . . . Grind sister. Girl's loins right in there. Kwa suk'amaphepha. Colossal sounds would leap out of those tiny pennywhistles to bathe our passions in the spirit of this moment far away from the slime of narrow, very rarely paved township streets.

This does not mean that New Year's celebrations gave birth to what critics in South Africa have called kwela or pennywhistle jazz. The refusal to forsake laughter, the dogged determination to survive in a society gone insane, the unrelenting love for dance and song, among innumerable other things in the townships, gave birth to this music. You see, this is not just dance music. This music is many things among which, as Ezekiel Mphahlele once pointed out, ". . . is a kind of sacrifice, an assertion. . . . coming straight from the anvil on which human emotions come under the endless hammering of the day's experiences."

European refugees in South Africa have turned practically every African who wishes to survive there into some kind of prostitute. At a very early age African boys have to learn to live by their wits. At nine when pretty often all they have to go home to for dinner is a few slices of bread and jam, they have to hustle for a few pennies to buy fish crumbs from some fish and chips shop which would, anywhere else in the world, throw them away. So in South African cities like Johannesburg, one finds boys ranging from about nine to early teens penny-whistling and dancing in white suburb sidewalks and entrances to train stations to catch a few pennies from whites enthralled by the agility of "pickaninnies." So we get together, we buy, steal or borrow some pennywhistles, we get a wooden box that is not too heavy for us to carry around, we make a small hole in the box and insert a string through the hole and we have a pennywhistle band with a self-made, one-string bass. No matter what your turn of mind, the lyricism and the sometimes bluesy anguished happiness of this seemingly casual music touches your sensibility. This music, sometimes robust, at times whining, always brutally moving and demanding, has all the ingredients of township life. Traditional tribal rhythms mingle freely with township demands, West African highlife, Afro-american jazz and rhythm-'n-blues to produce a distinctly South African sound in popular music.

The birth of the pennywhistle sound in South African music was around the late 'forties. The wizard who mothered it in recording studios was Willard Cele, now very seldom talked about. Since Cele there have been many other people, among them "Little" Lemmy and Spokes Mashiyange, who have filled and continue to fill the coffers of South African recording companies while they remain penniless. Generally the musicians do not get royalties from the sales of their records. If they did, people like Miriam Makeba, inimitable Dorothy Masuka and the uncrowned queen of South African blues Dolly Rathebe, among others, would have been filthy rich a long time ago. Lesser known names find themselves acting like third-rate prostitutes. A thousand times over one sees them outside recording studios, playing their lives away on the pavement to attract someone's attention in the studio. If they are lucky, they are called into the studio. They cut a record. They get a few pounds (now rand) -- not enough to buy one decent meal every day for a week -- and that is the end of the commercial potential of their talent.

Mbaqanga has grown fast since its birth on records. Now very often a guitar, drums and a regular bass are added to the ensemble. Often instead of they penny-whistle there is a sax or a trumpet. Voices are also very common and popular -- the lyrics the best poetry coming out of South Africa today -- at random they plunge into any aspect of our life; they speak of bus boycotts, of abandoned love affairs, they speak of the hideous pass system, of our exile in sanctuaries outside of South Africa where we dream and rehearse our death, where we humiliate and castrate ourselves. They are even bold enough to speak of revolution and be banned by those racist maniacs in South Africa.

* A dam North-east of Johannesburg (between Johannesburg and Pretoria) where we go for a picnic every New Year's Day.

Willie
Kgositsile

NEW GRASS/ALBERT AYLER

Personnel: Albert, tenor sax; Call Cobbs, piano, Electric Harpsichord and Organ; Bill Folwell, Electric bass; Pretty Purdie Drums, Burt Collins, Joe Newman Trumpets; Seldon Powell, tenor sax and flute, Buddy Lucas, baritone sax; Garnett Brown, Trombone.

Albert Ayler is one of the driving genuises of the Music. He has clearly put forth a definite sound; a different and fascinating way of thinking about the world as sound; as movement; as the ghostly memory of the Spiritual Principle. Albert's sound at its best is the field holler and the shout stretched like a piercing shaft from Alabama cotton fields to New York, and on into some cosmic world of strange energies. At his best, Albert's voices buzz and hum with awesome deities.

When most of us first heard Albert, he really blew our minds, opening us up to not only new possibilities in music, but in drama and poetry as well. He was coming straight out of the Church and the New Orleans funeral parades. He had all kinds of Coon songs in his horn. He had compressed, in terms of pitch, all of the implied cycles in the blues continuum. His thrust was shattering. So that we must acknowledge that anything we say about this album must be seen against Albert's fantastic possibilities.

But lately Albert's music seems to be motivated by forces that are not at all compatible with his genius. There is even a strong hint that the brother is being manipulated by Impulse records. Or is it merely the selfish desire for popularity in the american sense?

At any rate, this album is a failure. It attempts to unite rhythm and blues dynamic with the energy dynamic of Ayler. But in attempting to unite the two styles certain very fundamental things have been overlooked. First, rhythm and blues is rooted in a popular tradition which has allowed for innumerable innovations in and of itself. It is a tradition that demands respect. Men like Jr. Walker demand respect. Because like Bird, they are the masters of a particular form. Therefore, any contemporary musician who attempts to use R & B elements in his music should check out the masters of that form.

Like it's not too cool to get to the Rolling Stones or The Grateful Dead to learn things that your old man can teach you. And this is the feeling that I get from listening to New Grass. I mean the direct confrontation with experience as lived by the artist himself is not there. And this is a painful thing for me to say cause I have always dug Albert. I know what the Brother is trying to do. But his procedure is fucked up.

The rhythm on this album is shitty. There are no shadings, no implied values beyond the stated beat. The guitar is shitty. Most of the singing is shitty, especially the songs "Heart Love," and "Everybody's Moving." The Sister sounds like she is straining, trying to find some soul in a dead beat. There are no kinds of nuianees on the drums. Hard rock, death chatterings. Albert should check out Jr. Walker's band, or Bobby Blue Bland's rhythm section. He should dig the long version of James Brown's "There Was a Time." He should note the heavy spiritual blueness in the bass guitar. He should dig how the rhythm and blues people embellish the beat, how they use space.

All this information is immediate. Most of the good bands come through the Appollo. This is where the discovery must take place, not in the context of white rock. This album strains at everything, even social consciousness.

But Albert's attempt is fundamentally correct. It just must be focused sharper. The music must find ways of reaching into the pulse of the people; ways of taking ordinary elements out of their lives and reshaping them according to new principles. In this procedure, therefore, the music moves us toward national unity and spiritual unity. A Unity Music. A music that is so total, so fully informed by a Black ethos that it meets a more collective and less specialized need. Music can be one of the strongest cohesives towards consolidating the Black Nation. The music will not survive locked into bullshit categories. James Brown needs to know Albert Ayler, Sun Ra, Cecil Taylor, and Pharoah Sanders. I would like to see the Dells("Stay in My Corner"), with Pharoah or Archie Shepp. Implied here is the principle of artistic and national unity; a unity among musicians, our heaviest philosophers, would symbolize and effect a unity in larger cultural and political terms. Further, there should be more attempts to link the music to other areas of the Black Arts movement.

LIKE: REVOLUTIONARY CHOREOGRAPHERS LIKE ELEO POMARE, JOHN PARKS, JUDI DEARING, TALLY BEATY SHOULD BE CHECKING OUT CECIL TAYLOR'S MUSIC WHICH IS HEAVILY POSITED ON DANCE CONCEPTS.

****

HOW DOES POETRY AND MUSIC OPERATE IN THE CONTEXT OF POLITICAL AND RELIGIOUS GATHERINGS?

****

PHAROAH NEEDS A TEMPLE.

SUN RA IS A BEAUTIFUL BLACK INSTITUTION.

****

POETS SHOULD WRITE SONGS

****

And so on, Back to Albert. The so-called New Music represents at the core of its emanations the philosophical search of Black people for Self-definition. Unlike the blues, its placement is more directed at our possibilities in the cosmic sense. Every aspect of the music can feed on the other. There are still a myriad of possibilities for musicians in the area of the human voice. Max Roach and Donald Byrd showed the way: and there is still a lot of space left as Coltrane, Pharoah, and Albert indicate.

There are some profound possibilities in the area of tribal chorus. (Check out volume two (2) of the *World Library of Folk and Primitive Music*, Columbia, KL-205.) But these possibilities, as relevant as they are, will not be realized if we approach them as gimmicks adopted from jive white boys. What we will get in that case will be bull-shit "universalism."

Albert you are already universal. You were universal when you cut *My Name is Albert Ayler*; and even there the context was bad. Swedish nightmares. If you speak to your Brothers and Sisters, to us who really love, and care not just for you, but for us, you will be in fact universal. Check out your context black musicians. Who is your *primary* audience? Ed Sullivan, Janis Joplin, timothy leary ....? Or are you about something that relates to us; and even though we be slow in digging you sometimes, just the fact of you being nearby, around the corner; we all working it out together, reaching for that Unity Form; just this fact alone deepens communication and strengthens in a concrete spiritual manner.

GREAT SPIRITS, HELP US TO SEE AND HEAR

ASANTE

Larry Neal

ROCKGROUP

Cast

4 boys in whiteface

Beetle suits and wigs

Geetahs

(Background of psychedliquesence -- twang potsof odor)

A chained nigger (in falling down konk and raggidy sequined stage evening clothes)

VOICE -- "Ladies and gentlemen, tonight, for the first time on any stage, THE CRACKERS!!!

White boys come out, set up, go thru their motions. Bring something wiggling under a cloth, and hook up their instruments to it. (Can be mime or actual guitars, they plug in, all four.) Then set to play.

Song

White shit white shit white shit
hocuspocus in the clouds allright
White shit white shit white shit
hocuspocus in the clouds allright
Thass cool we got you fools everywhere
Thass cool we got hair in our chair we sit so tight

White shit white shit white shit
hocuspocus in the clouds allright

God and jesus is white fags smelling glue in
niggers shoes ooohooo white shit white shit white shit
hocuspocus in the clouds allright
hocuspocus in the clouds allright
hocuspocus in the clouds allright
hocuspocus in the clouds allright
...ahheyayayay

(They finish and bow, hair streaming wilding in they face. All the time they been going through they shit, black cloth been bumpin up and down wiggling and occasional when they the Crackers stop, low moans come out like something being beat

4WB- Thank you ladies and gentlemen. Thank you for digging us so tough.
VOICE-- "Ok lets hear it, folks, for THE CRACKERS ...
4WB- Thankyou ladies and gentlemen. Thankyou screams our tiny fag hearts...Yessssss
(Keep bowing to deafening applause and cheers, plant people in audience to cheer, plus tapes to increase sound to noise of madison square garden !!! YEEEEEEAAAAAAA)

Dudes keep bowing till sounds fades, some crazy white bitches run up and kiss them and make wierd conversation. Chontza Bing Doop?

Curry Cramp Vontz slappy.

Wobblyfink shumpish goink!

(They kiss and fondle, rip off grey clothes. They go thru they act being charming as piranas sucking on meat icecubes. Dainty and faggish and removed from reality swaggering like toygirls.)

Finally the set is over. Dollars have floated from the sky dropped by a big cardboard white hand from makebelieve cracker-heaven flying out of they god nose like bloody buggers

They gather up money tiredly, carting it off to they cave. The lights are going down slowly and quietly, as the crackers begin packing up their instruments. Then they uncover black cloth and unplug their instruments from out of this slumped over niggers behind he being laid out in silver conk and brown tuxedo. Crackers unplug the instruments, and put the nigger in a big velvet box marked "H I- V O L T A G E".

Just before they close the nigger in they put a toy car a half of a dollar bill, some white powder which he sniff and do funny things, then one of the white boys put on a lady outfit, and kiss him on lips, then nigger, he swoon dead away in box, and white boys carry him off with them.

As lights dim, big voice come on again, say; "LETS HEAR IT AGAIN FOLKS, FOR THE CRACKERS" (MAD CRAZINESS OF LOUD YELLS AND STUFF DIGGING THEM DIGGING THEM DIGGING THE HELL OUT OF THEM)

IMAMU AMEER BARAKA

LIBERATION

[TO LE GRAHAM]

My soul
was tied to
a decaying
Hollywood
of insanity -
out of tune
& mind
until the
Liberation
of my
Blackness.

Coltrane
taught me
what it was
to be
Black.
Coltrane,
Shepp,
Taylor
taught me
how
to be.

My mind
untill
the
Liberation
of my
Blackness
was jagged
with
20th Century
madness.

My Blackness
came
like
fire-poems
from
Le Graham
&
Jones
came
like
fire-music
from
Ayler
&
Monk
My Blackness
came
like
chaos
on
surburban blocks
came

like

4th of July

    Hysteria.

My soul

My mind

My Blackness

Liberated

Emancipate

from

bourgeois apathy

from

main-stream make-believe

from

western ways of seeing.

Coltrane,

Shepp,

Taylor,

Ayler,

Monk,

Le Graham

   &

  Jones

Emancipated

Liberated

My Blackness

set me free

in blazing dawns

    of truth.

E. Hill

NOTES ON LOU DONALDSON & ANDREW HILL

("Say It Loud" Blue Note BST84299)
(E "GrassRoots" Blue Note 84303 w/the mixmatched kids on the cover and the moneymusic inside)

Lou-
Soul music does not mean weak music, Lou Donaldson. Say it Loud, in its take off here is made simple minded and imaginationless. James Brown in his work is neither The only musician right now on general records who gets to the subtleties, harmonics, and fire at the same time as JB is of course, Pharoah.

To say that Lou perhaps is simple minded in that he takes R & B for something "less complicated" than jazz. Which is stupid. Check it out. Imitate Otis Redding <u>You don't miss your water</u> with a piano, new piano man, and see where you come out harmonically !!!! Fahamu???

Andrew (& others)
RealRoot is the <u>return</u> necessary. The eternal verities of your naturalness. So Andrew Hill, "aging", has decided his realroot is the social facility of american illusion, as it was at another period of his (our) lives. You can not lie to your self, after a time. Only the absolute devil can do this, the joke of course, being that the lie is itself the evil.

We are speaking of "going back" to wakefulness. From sleep. Going back to what is better, not relaxing into the obscurity of one section of the dead.
+++
What is necessary is constant effort at achieving a total. At achieving something New. Make it New attributed to Ezra Pound is Eastern. It is the African (and Sufi) explanation of why life, even though contained by an endless cycle, or not contained, <u>is</u> an endless cycle can be, is worthwhile, i.e. make it new and lo and behold KARMA (digit???)

Imamu Ameer Baraka

Between Shadow And Substance-Part I

How does one try to begin to put together the Black music scene in a city like Paterson when the whole black cultural esthetic is out of perspective--almost non-existant except for a few dedicated black musicians, one of whom is Terry Lee who refuses to have his stupendous talents prostituted by the local club owners, mostly white.

Paterson has the peculiar habit of being able to produce some strong musicians and today is no exception, however, our problem like most of the larger cities e.g. N.Y., Chi., Det., etc. is proper exposure in an atmosphere that is conducive to both playing and listening and if as Brother Spellman points out Black music is a part of the culture in the vanguard of the struggle then its time to get busy and put together an atmosphere in which these musicians can create the proper images and provide a direction for the youth of today. For without this creativity today we face a directionless void that will be difficult to fill in future years.

Getting back to Terry Lee. When the opportunity arises and we get a chance to hear Terry then we know that we have come upon a large oasis of Black music in a vast desert of nothingness and to drink of this music is so refreshing that we momentarily forget the emptiness that was there. Terry Lee is an Afro Drummer of extrodinary talents who hails originally from Cleveland and Paterson has truly been blessed to have him settle here. Terry has been teaching and playing for the last few years and has developed a core of fine young musicians that are truly a pleasure to hear.

What influences his playing and provides the drive and impetus for his music? Ask him and he will tell you that they range from ancient African rythums, through the rythums developed by the Moors who traveled from Spain to settle in Latin America, to the new black music that is now being created by all the brothers in North America.

Paterson certainly needs black musicians of Terry's calibre and the black people of the area should avail themselves of these cats thereby providing the kind of support they need to continue their work.

Writer's note:

The title for this article was taken from the last chapter of Harold Cruse's book "The Crises of the Negro Intellectual" which is considered a must reading for all black cultural revolutionaries. This article and all future articles by this writer will endeavor to provide some substance for the shadow that exists.

SALAAM

RONNIE GROSS

REVOLUTIONARY BLACK MUSIC FOR THE REVOLUTIONARY BLACK PEOPLE AT THE EAST COFFEE—HOUSE/RAPPA HOUSE ON DETROIT'S EAST SIDE

Somewhere in the nite Black musicians gather to form guerrilla warfare and put down the supreme effort/war, to the liberation of Black people. One of the houses that has started out of the collectiveness and love for Black people and there music is East Coffee-House, 285 E. Ferry, between John R. & Brush, is right in the heart of Det.'s 2nd oldest (hastings being the 1st, which has been destroyed by the in-hateful fisher freeway) Black community. It sits behind one of these big old mansions that have been chopped into hotels or one of the many Black fraternity/sorority houses. A garage-tenement house is somewhere in the nite that has begun screaming but needs the support of Black people, revolutionary Black people and the revolutionary Black musicians and their groups in the struggle being waged. This music of life by the spirit vibrators scream the message of their souls. Art/revolutionary Black music hangs on the walls as Otis Bey's group terrorizes the racists or Jimmy Morgan playing the dreams of Black people . . .

Otis Bey/leader of one baddest, loven & guts to say it groups comes from the guerrilla war zone of Cleveland, Ohio. He has been living and trying to work here for the past 2 years on mastering his guns/alto, soprano and tenor sax. A self-taught Black musician and feels that his music must state that here it comes the time is now/we've done all that one can... say it now that all those who wait, you get it!

Ahemed Abdul/drums is a monster and states it in a hard bizarre movement that he stays in control of...all about music/Black revolutionary music to liberate Black people. Certain types of Black music that should be called Original Music--you can feel that he draws strength from the innovator Bey in that it is energy for revolution. A design that puts out the message...ITS NOT NEW. Sun Ra was doing it long ago. Other thoughts on the members has touched the young vibrator but the feeling is one the bassist Kenneth Milliner who is trying to get something concrete/away from the abstract feeling of the western orientalism of jazz. Charles Eubanks/piano also from burnings. Charles Miles/alto sax and flute "C"... a circle of communication to Black people to present the love of Blackness and the spirit-cosmic non western theroid music. Adbus Aba/pocket trumpet plays the way he feels as a captured Black man. His seizure of power in un-blocking the emotionless expression of brainwashed - jazz...to play violently toward the Devils.

Poet in residence Maliki Bey blows the lines/guerrilla warfare and Blackism. It's an effort to reach people/true revolutionary Black people, thru all art forms in order to hook-up all vibrations in making JAHED...supreme effort/war/to the liberation of Black people all over the world.

Jimmy Morgan will drown your tears and stretch your soul back on the path of dreams of nationhood/of life, the things you can't see but hear will be interviewed in another inquiry.

The Rappa House is where you do enjoy the finest in jazz and dining on that soul Creole cooking. Located in the downtown area on the new street/fisher freeway between woodward and John R. 96 E. Fisher Freeway. The main group is Hal McKenny who makes you think of Cecil Taylor the way he controls the sounds you hear from the piano. Psychologically when Teddy Harris blows his soprano sax with Hal they succeed in making you understand the swiftness of the revolutionary Black music, the walls report the importance of liberation. Isac Delany/drummer who does things that burns a purity of tension, on higher, higher/until - rattttatr staccate of machine guns firing!!! Bro' Terry Moore on Bass brings the four Bros' together in a controlled sense of original Black music/an expression of his revolution...being the leaders of the revolutionary vanguard.

From 2 A.M. - 6 A.M. the most remarkable sounds are heard for you to listen to make you un-ignorant of the life force and teach the crushed that there is no fear in death...never love life more than your people.

Ibn Pori 'det.

HARLEM COLUMN #2

"Monday night at Basie's".
It's black-owned, now, they say.
Inside I stood a few moments,
then I bought the required drink (a beer)
Charles Tyler was ending a set.
He sounds like Ornette Coleman,
or Ornette sounds like him,
or they sound like each other.
The drummers were fantastic.
They played old rhythms
to the new melodies
of this music that developed
outside of Harlem.
It'll probably change if it stays here.
The people's reactions will influence the musicians.
The people react to the drummers
strength and drive
but are more receptive to the
foot-tapping rhythms behind
the unusual (to most of Basie's usual crowd)
sounds that come from the horns.
I like Charles Tyler's playing -

I wonder what you'll think.

He knows his instrument well-enough to play

exactly what he wants to say -

no rhythmic inspiration seems too great

for him to play with/over/under/around/on/ahead/etc.

Don Ayler played some of what he knew

and he wasn't trying, but doing!

A display of strength (spiritual, mental, physical)

that impressed and inspired me.

Hearing music fulfills one of my needs.

I hope next Monday's as strong.

ben caldwell

JULIUS LESTER

Brother Julius Lester has just now released a second lp, Departures, on Vanguard. In it he shows several shades of beauty, all Black; some ballads, some folksongs, several blues. Nine of the 10 songs are original, which, in the general context of this man's life, tells us something about this brother's energy quotient. He is one of the very best writers that we have with a militant column in the National Guardian with two books coming out from Dial: Look Out Whitey, Black Power's Gonna Get Your Mamma, and a collection of children's stories from Africa. He is an accomplished photographer and a SNCC worker and an editor at Sing Out Magazine.

I believe that Julius is essentially a writer who has extended his expressive apparatus to new forms. Yes, he sings quite well, being gifted with a deep, resonant bass voice, and he plays good guitar. But I listen to these songs first for what Julius says and then for how he says it. Not that the two are separable, but you'd pick Julius' Stago Lee (on Julius Lester, the earlier Vanguard release) over Wilson Pickett's or Lloyd Price's, not because Julius sings better but because his Stago is such an evil nigger that he digs death as just another whitey and pulls a gun on him and then when he gets to hell he attends a barbecue of hunkie meat.

Lester obviously directs his music to young Black people, and they certainly would dig it if they could get to it. But white-controlled public media are not set up to disseminate revolutionary Black music. They are set up to brainwash and not to enlighten, and so Julius' talking blues, Dressed Like Freedom, will never be the hit it should be. Here Lester conducts a dialogue between two soul brothers, one with an Afro and a lot of Black consciousness, and the other with neither. Viz: "Hey man, D's looking for you." "D who?" "D barber, nigger." The 'froed brother then goes on to "educate" his friend. "There once was a time when I was ashamed of being Black. But since I been dressed like freedom, all the white folks are getting back." Lester turns an image around on the hunkie: "white folks and flies, lord I do dispise. But the more I see white folks, oooh, the more I like flies."

Several of the blues are informed by Lester's experience as a SNCC worker in the south. He will not die a one-sided death as so many of our people have; he will take a hunkie with him: "If I get killed down south, I want a white boy by my side. So won't nobody say just another nigger done died." Others are full of the rats and roaches that the oppressor keeps so close to power in his house that they yell "freedom now" whenever he gets close to them. While he uses the same melody in all his blues, the lyrics are deep excavations into the condition and conditioning of his people that extend without altering the blues tradition, as when the landlord of the Landlord Blues told him, "Nigger, if you don't like it here, you can move to the other side of town. He knows I can't live there, cause over there they got grass growing out the ground."

A together record altogether. Cop.

- Donald Stone

PHIL COHRAN - AFFRO ARTS THEATER

Bro. Cohran a former Sun-Ra trumpet player has soul shown in cosmic music with blood prints beating. (A Blood Prince, himself, beating all into Spirit). Grass Roots Ra is what it is. Singing, Like Ra, but on an earth plane nationalist oriented & beautiful because it's there and we sho need it. RA'S RAYS ARE TRANSLATED INTO HIPPISH NATIONAL ANTHEMS.

But it is more than just that, the boogalooish earthiness is a self reality splendid as it self w/o reference to any other being. (But all beings come from a being).

Cohran is important past his past. He exists beautiful like he is, with the consciousness, also, to produce his own sides. A Black Reality. To have a Black theater. A Black necessity. The contemporary Black man moving for himself, independent, as opposite to Shaitan, on an opposite path.

We must celebrate our selves, our large selves. Our holy Blackness!

Discography: Zulu Records

Philip Cohran, & the Artistic Heritage Ensemble

w/Cohran, Frankiphone (An amplified sanza, or thumb piano)

Cornet, Violin Uke

Pete Cosey, Guitar

Charles Handy, Trpt. & Chinese Musette

Steven Galloway, Trombone

Master Henry Gibson, Conga and Timbales

Eugene Easton, Tenor Sax, Flute and Oboe

Donald Myrick, Baritone and Tenor Sax

Bob Crowder, Jr., Trap Drums

Louis Satterfield, Bass and Trombone

Charles James Williams, Alto Sax

Aaron Dodd, Tuba

Mrs. Ella Pearl Jackson, Vocal

Patricia Smith, Vocal

Imamu Ameer Baraka

CHARLES E CLARK:

SUDDENLY THE BLUES

heard with
richard abrams &
joseph jarman on
bass & cello

born march 11, 1945
diéd
april 15, 1969
only
the living
wear mask

----Roger----Riggins

RECORD REVIEW - YOUR PRAYER

Your Prayer (ESP-Disk 1053) by Frank Wright (Frank Wright, tenor & buffet sax; Arthur Jones, alto; Jacques Coursil, trumpet; Steve Tintweiss, bass; Muhammad Ali, drums)

Frank Wright takes me completely out everytime I hear him. He's definitely one of the heaviest players to emerge on the scene since Trane--this brother is mean! Brother Wright represents one of the most advanced or natural playing styles in the new Black music (and when I speak of style I'm talking about conceptual ideology not just facility and all that crap).

Brother Wright also chooses his companions well. They understand this music--they are this music, pure to itself. They are brothers involved in Black creation. They are Black priest shouting sweet turded reality clusters to US.

All of the tracks were good but some I felt were excellent. The excellent ones being The Lady and the title tune Your Prayer. The Lady by altoist Arthur Jones (watch for this cat, he'll tear your head right off) is a real theme and variation piece--but it is not a "tune" in the conventional sense because at times (especially when Frank starts to TCB) the players go beyond connection of theme to perpetuate a variation. As musician-writer James Stewart said to me, "Wha I do at the beginning of a piece has really nothing to do with what comes after." Your Prayer is even less a composition. It is deeper than Lady. I mean the concept it was conceived out of was deeper, a more socially aware idea of creation. Muhammad is into some very real energy on this track and Frank is unusually strong on this cut too--tongue slaps on reed--even and intense flow of energy--passionate screams and shouts--the beauty of the cosmos opened up. The rest of the group is also on a wild Black trip on this track. Space is where we are, outer space is where we're going.

Check out Brother Frank Wright, he might teach you something horribly true about yourself.

---Roger Riggins---

GOSSIP

(Note from Cleveland)

"As-Salaam-Alakium, may Allah, Lord of the Worlds, find you in peace. We The Black Unity Trio, (who have, recently, released Al-Fatihah on Salaam Records, Stereo 777-A. The group is made up of Yusef Mumin, Alto Sax; Ron DeVaughn, Cello and Bass; Haasan-Al-hut, Percussionist) welcome a free exchange of ideas and will assist you in any way possible. We were once The Cleveland United Black Artists. This group even had a well to do Black offer to purchase a place for cultural expansion of the arts, but most of the members were lost and the others were too weak or indifferent.

Anyway that has dried up some little funny conflict. The music here is far behind in time, no place for new music. Most people here think we are nuts (true). Most musicians have lost interest, and fallen into the same old dope - pit. Narco seems to be the most important thing, nobody really wants to play new music. If there is, we can't find them and our vibration is out there, address and all. But, all praises to Allah, we ain't New York crazy either. We hope Brother that you enjoy the message in Al-Fatihah and hope you'll enjoy Mystic Visions which will be out in eight weeks. You will be one of the first to receive a copy. We will keep in touch; enjoyed the Cricket. Wa-Salaam-Alakium, The Black Unity Trio"

(The Cricket, answers Asante for all the praise. Keep playing, your message is in our hearts. The body, nation, is coming together - head, arms, legs, nervous system and all. It will function Black forever.) Al-Fatihah can be obtained by writing these brothers at 12715 Superior, Cleveland, Ohio. You should do it right now, 'fore all the white freaks buy them, stealing for days. Warming themselves off your bodyheat.

Black Unity Trio says "Mystic visions of divine expressions of the cosmos that expand music beyond itself and enables it to indicate by emotional intensity what it cannot clearly express." They say that "Music is the song of the universe. All people have symbols that only they understand, but some form of music is understood by every soul. Certain mentalities can absorb only certain vibrations, but no matter how small the effort, it contains a light of spiritual; and each part has its place and predetermined existence. Degrading people may use it, but music cannot be degrading, it is divine in every form. In the force of this music, the knowledge of the true universe has been caught in a vibration of energy to teach, to heal and to bring joy.

The music of the universe is a live wire of energy. The rhythms and the sounds instantly illuminate a flash of cosmic power. Say "BE" and behold it is".

(The sharpest black blessings are sent to these bad dudes, from us. They are our brothers. We praise them in the highest. This music is what we need, and more in and outside of this. Hum this tune, "Birth, Life, and Death" and the rest like them forever.)

(San Fran)

"I'm going to try to get together an article about Black Music in San Francisco --- something historical, analytical, down, but I have to get to the right people first --- like Jimbo, who owned Bop-City, and who probably met and got to know every Black Musician who came this way. Got to go peace.

(The quick words, from Joe Goncalves, editor/publisher of Journal of Black Poetry, read it!)

(Newark)

First of all it's hard to believe that there is any comment from Newark, and maybe you ain't even ready for it. But maybe you is, cause here it is. Stacy Edwards, conga drummer, former Olatunji man, recently finished a two month gig with Marvin Gaye (I Heard it Thru the Grapevine, Good Lovin' Ain't Easy to Come by, Too Busy Thinkin 'Bout my Baby,etc.) Last date together was the Appollo Theater/ Edwin Starr also, on the program (Back Street, SOS). He tough also, doodoodoo, people say, yeah. They always saying, your name off they lips. Now Stacy said, coming out of the First and Last African Shop, 123 Clinton Place, Newark, "got to get ready to make a date with the Temptations at the White House, for Nixon's daughter". Ain't dat a bitch. She sho is. See how we light their lights. They only survive with straws in they mouth suck suck suckin on your energy digging you. Wbs trying to bring themselves back to life. Never happen. He now don't know about cab driving any mo, but dn't forget.

Sun Ra, The World's Greatest Musician, played at 502, The Committee for Unified Newark Audience in March, filled all the space in the room with magic, played and spoke of his "presence", swings, swung from when he created them. Blackman with all the beauty in the world outside the world due him. Just recently finished tour of California. (Besides, Sun Ra, Pharoah Sanders, The Black Unity Trio and other young musicians along this line of feeling/energy playing so they can be heard or anything new, just "hip" stuff, there are no musicians. Voices, all bow to Leon Thomas who by now has been heard if you haven't, don't let music talk drop from your lips till you do. All the strongness of Egyptian air breathes thru him, the creators vessel, star. Man this dude is bad and we been talking about him for some time (he jumped from Count Basie to Pharoah with his own groups in between, bird singing). Can you dig Nazakat and Salamat Ali, two brothers terrible terrible (chant)ers from Pakistan. They bees. Can you dig it, naw you cant devil, never, dem dudes blows you shit every time. Ha ha. The label is Odeon for all those with ears, untouched by rocks and stones (bullshit cheap death), that can hear. And fit into their fullness.

The Committee for Unified Newark, in its series of Black Arts/Soul Culture goings on. BMIE has had some dopey ones too, for instance, Donald Ayler played there. With his murphy game shoutin thru the shit he was sayin on stage, drunk, zipper open, staggering, he call his self a musician. Really just a cheap version with no identity, purpose and direction; nigger lacks. A value system. Right and wrong. Good and bad. Up and down. In and out. Up on stage with Bee ber Harris, who white wee moans, dun sucked about all his juice/energy from him insides. Slobin on his self. Unconscious of who he is or where he is going. Has no value system. Umoja, nia, kuumba (unity, purpose, creativity) and the rest. Laws that you live your life by, unchanging, good. Came to New Ark "playing" in this quick trio put together by Ayler, (who has since, said Sonny Murray, gone back to his hometown Cleveland to re cooperate, re gather, hopefully come back, BLACK). Which had on the first night on Indian oboe, (due to bullshit reasons) said his trumpet was stolen, and wanted to borrow our alto sax.; he did and broke it. We had to suffer, his "playing" one beatup note all night, which would have probably been the same on alto. Next night they came back Ayler had a trumpet which he said the "spirit brought to him" and played the same big ass run, the whole set. While in his rhythm section Richard Davis, bass, had the only strong sound anyone there could use. BH, slobbered and nodded on his drums in a dopey daze, rocking back and forth to a crazy image of some dead white bitch. Splash! was his sound the whole night.

Sunny Murray, and his Spiritual Sextet, sounded good on their visit. And all the hopes for the best future. Arthur Jones, alto sax, (will be heard from) was playing with Sunny this night and climbing over what Ornette has put out here faster than light. (Find them and give them some money.) Who ever got it to give. Bro name Jumba, was playing drums with another bro Ali, the two together had hands so fast it sounded like a tribe and thunder mixing up gold dust. Alan Shorter, trumpet player was there, made a dumb statement after playing a tune sounding like a page of Sun Ra, "An we aint africans neither". A value system. No other way. It has to be. So we can BE. Sunny working with lead, chorus, tune. Quinn Lynch his tenor man, provides the intros. The group it self, Sunny Murray, drum leader, Arthur Jones, Alto sax., Jumba, Bass, congas, Alan Shorter, trumpet, Quinn Lynch, tenor sax. Ali, Basoon, flutes and congas. Fast instructive energy each minute they speak. Tho Shorter sounded as if he was waiting for something/one to fill him up. Other than the beer cup they had floating around on stage. values. Again it can never be gotten away from. The ones they have now are no good for them, they are the insides of a dead sore. Meanwhile Murray keeping all the space filled to the top with his moannnnnnnsss and groannnnnnnsss. The tunes sound like what spirits, manifest, as. Worth sitting there listening (but even before that feeling) its master, the cosmo dude next to me kept wanting me to see the musicians. Tho it was only about the sound, feeling, sweeping thru (energy, heat) they heads. The Creators willing to let beauty be. In a being(s). The stops, slows. Fast changes. Drags, up, fast. Filling, moans, all space.

More, Black Music in Evolution at the Committee audience has been Pharoah Sanders and Leon Thomas, with them were Roy Brooks, drums, Norris Jones, bass, Lonnie L. Smith, Jr., piano. They played Upper and Lower Egypt, Pharoah, screaming wildly. On to spirit, with drifts of gospel, funkee, earth mixed all close to it. Roy Brooks, entertained w/his soft thumb piano solo which set up Norris Jones for his, bass solo. Then Pharoah "arrived" after we all had missed him. Making the whole (church) move. See See Rider, Full Spirit, of the holy Blackman (Pharoah-Leon) in the air. Everybody rocked, back and forth feeling good. The Spirit was inside us. Pharoah started dancing, and we camel walked. Images of red and green turn up in your heart warm Sun. Pointing constantly past, what is seen or felt, turn it into light. Heavy nigger conversations on Howard St. The sound (s), hums, moans. All these together. The experience of Blackman in this country from past, present, and future. The finders, innovators, reach for. All in one wave. The self with others. Working for your nation, your music club. Don't want to play in somebody else's, want muh own club, record company. Can you dig it?

For all times, These beings are priests, creators of (all) that breathes, new looking cities. Pharoah Sanders, James Brown, Jr. Walker, Sun Ra, Leon Thomas, Spirit House Poets in they old reading days had what everybody has picked up on to use. Voices, music, motion, chants in the dark. The beginning. When will they come back with it again stretched out beyond that?

THE CRICKETS

AIDE DENIES LBJ CALLED POPE "A DUMB CUNT"

A high government source termed "completely unfounded" a report made by the Japanese newspaper, Sokitoomi, that President Johnson called Pope Paul "A dumb cunt".

The incident reportedly took place last month when the President conferred with the Pontiff on the deteriorating situation in Southeast Asia.

The newspaper went on to report that, "LBJ stalked the room like a spooky longhorn," and warned the leader of world Catholics that if he ever visited Washington he'd better wear a "bullet proof skull cap".

A secret serviceman present during the Vatican meeting moved a finger across his throat and made a clicking sound with his tongue as if to emphasize the President's threat.

"The Pope got the message," Sokitoomi continued, because a scheduled March visit to Washington was indefinitely post-poned without explanation.

The incident, one of a series that was to mar the President's visit to Italy and further test the already strained relations between the White House and the Vatican, so enraged the Chief Executive that he fired the Italian Ambassador, George Fredrick Reinhardt.

Earlier, thousands of Italian anti-war protestors taunted the President's party with signs reading "Free LeRoi Jones", Down with Arthur Godfrey".

Mr. Johnson was allegedly angry with the Pope because he refused to declare him, "The Second Messiah".

Ishmael Reed

THERE

There is a land
Whose being is almost unimaginable to t
Human mind.
On a clear day,
We stand there and look farther than the
ordinary eye can see.
Far above the roof of the world,
We can encompass vistas of the worlds.

There is a land
Where the sun shines eternally . . .
Eternally eternal:
Out in outer space
A living blazing fire,
So vital and alive . . .
There is no need to describe its splendor.

The Cricket: Black Music in Evolution, 1968–69

Published by Blank Forms Editions
in Brooklyn, New York

The Cricket: Black Music in Evolution was published by Jihad Productions in four issues from 1968 to 1969 and edited by Amiri Baraka, Larry Neal, and A. B. Spellman. This volume collects all four issues as they were originally published.

Blank Forms Editions

Artistic Director: Lawrence Kumpf
Managing Editor: Ciarán Finlayson

Copyeditor: Dana Kopel
Design: Alec Mapes-Frances

Printed by Ofset Yapımevi in Istanbul, Turkey

ISBN 978-1-953691-10-1
First edition

Blank Forms would like to thank Parker Allen and Morgan Levine for their research assistance. Additional thanks are due to Pierre Crépon, C. Daniel Dawson, Christopher Funkhouser, Danielle A. Jackson, Evelyn Neal, Evan Neuhausen, Steve Rowland, Catherine Scott, Mutawaf A. Shaheed, Ron Welburn, and the following librarians: Okezie Amalaha and Derek Mosley, Auburn Avenue Research Library on African American Culture and History; Tom McCutchon, Columbia University; Christian Kelleher and Bethany Scott, University of Houston; Wendy Adams and Rachael Dreyer, Pennsylvania State University; Sarah Mouch, University of Toledo; Phillip Cunningham and Christopher Harter, Tulane University; Lori B. Bessler, Wisconsin Historical Society; and Rebecca Maguire, Yale University. The writing by Jimmy Stewart is reprinted here with the kind permission of his three children: Michael Stewart, Larklyn Stewart-Brown, and Wynton Stewart.

Blank Forms Editions is produced with support from the Robert Rauschenberg Foundation, the Andy Warhol Foundation for the Visual Arts, and Agnes Gund.

Blank Forms
468 Grand Ave, Unit 3D
Brooklyn, NY 11238
blankforms.org